CW01660113

Chelsfield Chronicles

Annals of a Kentish Parish

by Geoffrey Copus

Front cover illustration:
Chelsfield in 1910, etching by W.R. Cope of Orpington

Frontspiece illustration:
The Tree of Life, from a brass of c1470 in Chelsfield Church

Back cover illustrations by Randolph Caledott - Chelsfield
Characters from "The Owls of Olynn Belfrey" 1885

Published with the aid of a grant from the Local History Fund of the Kent Archeological Society

The publishers have made every effort to trace copyright holders and apologise for any unintentional errors or omissions.

Copyright 2003 CAT designs

Text copyright 2003 Geoffrey Copus

All rights reserved including the right of reproduction in whole or in part in any form.

The right of Geoffrey Copus to be identified as the author of this work has been asserted in accordance with Section 77 & 78 of the Copyright, Designs & Patents Act 1988 U.K.

ISBN 1 872886 01 9

Set in Bookman Old, 10 point. DTP by Carole Tyrrell

Printed by The Ink pot, Tunbridge Wells

CONTENTS

DEDICATION

To the memory of my father, Leslie Welch Copus, organist and choirmaster of St. Martin's, Chelsfield, from 1946 to 1959, and also of my mother Dorothy née Russum, who waited patiently for him.

Special acknowledgements

I should like to acknowledge the great help given to me by Bill Morton, the historian of Crofton. Over many years he has been very generous in copying photographs as well as providing much historical information of value, often from unexpected sources.

Susan Pittman, the historian of Crockenhill, has always been supportive as well as often exchanging research discoveries with me.

Paul and Denise Rason of Orpington for years encouraged me to publish a book on Chelsfield, and generously gave me my first computer, after which I had no excuse for further delay.

INTRODUCTION

As I was born in 1930 at Town Court Lane, in rural Orpington, and have never lived in Chelsfield, I owe an explanation for my passion for that parish. In 1946 my father Leslie Copus became organist and choirmaster of St. Martin's Chelsfield, and sometimes called on me to pump the organ, when I relieved the tedium by dipping into the bound volumes of old Parish Magazines, which were in the Vestry. The picture of village life glimpsed in their pages fascinated me, and I soon started the lifelong task of abstracting all the information about Chelsfield which I could find in documentary sources.

In 1949 I was given permission by Col. Henry Waring to transcribe such Chelsfield Manorial documents as I wished at the wonderfully Dickensian office of Dimonds, the family's solicitors, in Welbeck Street. This permission was later extended to Brenda Cooper, then my fiancée, and we happily worked there at intervals over the next few years.

I was fortunate to be encouraged in my interest by the late Arthur Eldridge of Orpington, a great local historian who taught me a lot. By 1951 I felt confident enough to put on quite an ambitious local history exhibition for St. Martin's church in the old Reading Room, as part of the Festival of Britain celebrations. One astonished visitor was Dennis Clarke, my history master at Chislehurst and Sidcup Grammar School - I had never shone at his subject.

Brenda Cooper and I were married at St. Martin's in 1953, and moved to Tunbridge Wells in 1960, and Chelsfield, although never forgotten, had to take a back seat until I retired in 1990. The book that I had intended to publish soon after that has been continually delayed as ever more documentation has become available.

I have not attempted to write anything like a full history of Chelsfield, but instead have expanded on a number of topics, which particularly interest me. In this I have been influenced by the example of the great Dr. Gordon Ward, whose "Sevenoaks Essays" seems to me to be a model of what a book on local history should be – based entirely on original research, scholarly and accurate but with a light touch that makes it interesting to the general reader. In my case, because little from the earlier Middle Ages has survived, the period covered is broadly 1450 to 1920.

It is difficult to find the ideal between too little and too much in the way of references. I trust that I would be able to justify any statements I have made, but so as not to over-burden the book I have not given exact references to some sources, such as Census returns and post-1858 wills. I have acknowledged in the text the names of people who over the years have given me information or lent me documents.

I believe it is a tremendous waste of the transcriber's time to make literal transcripts of documents. In this work, therefore, while retaining proper names and place names in their original form, I have generally modernised the spelling and punctuation. In only a few cases, which are clear in the text, that of the original has been retained.

Carole Tyrrell, who rashly volunteered to prepare the book for publication, has worked long hours with a firm but kind and enthusiastic hand to bring it to fruition. My wife has lived patiently with my obsession with Chelsfield ever since we met in 1949; a professional family historian and record agent herself, it was perhaps poetic justice that she should have discovered that her roots in the district lie far deeper than mine. Through her ancestor Charlotte Rolls, baptised at Farnborough in 1798, she is connected with a whole network of local families including those of French and Squibb.

She and I met Dr. Gordon Ward only once, at a Kent Archaeological Society meeting organised by Mrs. Piercy Fox of Keston in 1953. We kept a low profile among distinguished company, but Dr. Ward was very friendly, and when my wife told him that I was writing a parish history he commented with perfect truth – "My dear young lady, that will take him at least fifty years........."

Geoffrey Copus
Tunbridge Wells, Kent
September 2003

Chapter 1

CHELSFIELD IN 1914 – "THE NEW DOMESDAY BOOK"

"A few already in this year of Grace 1912 travel to London by Motor car – will this be the vehicle of the many in the near future?"

– Arthur Waring in his manuscript Chelsfield Parochial Notes

Arthur Waring, Lord of the Manor of Chelsfield, was an admirable local historian, and any successor must be grateful for the thoroughness and reliability of his Parochial Notes and transcripts. I picture him writing in the uninterrupted quietness of his study, basing the work largely on his own huge collection of deeds. In the village at that time things appeared to continue much as they had done for centuries, but in reality it was a period of rapid change, and the motorcar, detested by Mr. Waring, was only one manifestation of progress. With good reason, he and others of his class felt threatened by the Liberal Government's reforms, not least the Act introduced with a view to taxing the incremental value of land.

To this end, the Valuation Office initiated a survey of all property in the country, generating a huge volume of valuable information[1]. The Valuation Books, which earned the survey the title of "The New Domesday," list the names of owners and occupiers of houses and land, and much other detail. On the accompanying maps each property, whether a farm with hundreds of acres or a small cottage, is outlined in red and given a number. The numbers refer to the entries in the Valuation Books and in the third class of documents, the Field Books.

These books, compiled on the spot by the Valuation Office surveyors, generally give an estimated age for each building, the materials of which it was constructed, the number of rooms on each floor and whether it had main drainage, water,

gas and (rarely) electricity, and ground floor plans are sometimes included. The survey of Chelsfield began in 1910 and continued at intervals until late 1914, giving a wonderful picture of the parish on the eve of the Great War, an event which changed social conditions in such a decisive way.
The ancient parish contained 3218 acres, and stretched from close to Orpington church in the north to a point well beyond Cudham church in the south. In this brief survey of Chelsfield in 1914 I have looked in turn at the three main areas of the parish.

Chelsfield Village & Hamlets

Although much of this upper part of the parish was owned by Arthur Waring of Woodlands, there were other substantial holdings, among them Chelsfield House, the former Rectory (now Chelsfield Park Hospital) which belonged to Edward Norman, a partner in Martins Bank.

Woodlands had been built in 1815, and perhaps the only material improvement since that time was that water had been laid on; there was no gas or electricity, while drainage was still by means of a cesspool. Chelsfield House was built a little later than Woodlands, but the contrast between the two "big houses" of the village was very marked. Mr. Norman had added substantially to his property, and the surveyor is quite lyrical in his description of the house and grounds - " a charming Residential Estate embracing about 60 acres including a fine old Georgian Residence which has been enlarged and partly rebuilt and refitted in an expensive and thoroughly up to date manner including a new Electric light plant and new Stabling etc. The grounds are mostly park like lands and the whole Estate is well kept up and in exceptionally good order throughout." Among the other buildings on the estate were a lodge, coach house and stabling and glasshouses.

Down Skibbs Lane Hubert Blackwell, the village blacksmith had built for himself a house and forge on land belonging to Edward Norman, who let it to him on a 99-year lease from 1 June 1897 at £30 per annum. There was a brick coach-building house with a galvanised paint shop over it, while the forge itself is described as being "brick foundation galvanised

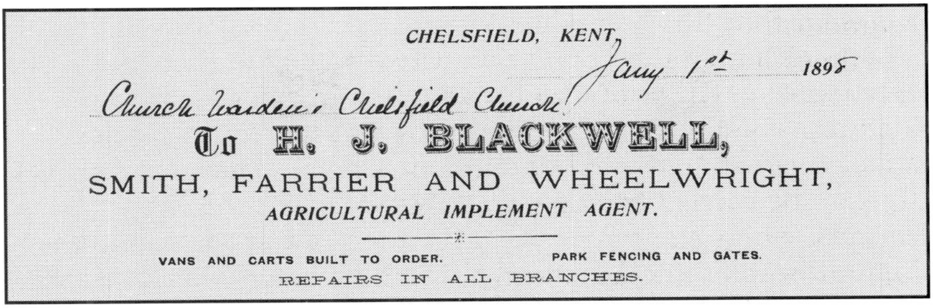
CHELSFIELD, KENT, Jany 1st 1895

Church Wardens Chelsfield Church

To H. J. BLACKWELL,

SMITH, FARRIER AND WHEELWRIGHT,

AGRICULTURAL IMPLEMENT AGENT.

VANS AND CARTS BUILT TO ORDER. PARK FENCING AND GATES.

REPAIRS IN ALL BRANCHES.

Letterhead of Hubert Blackwell, the blacksmith

and slated roof. "The other amenities, in the centre of the village, included the Five Bells, a Post Office and general store and two bakeries, while just up the hill at Rounds James Smith the builder and undertaker had his house, workshop and orchard. Arthur Thomas Verrells, the harness maker, left the village during the course of the four years which it took to complete the survey, perhaps the first sign of the gradual decline of the old self-contained community which has left it today with neither shop nor Post Office.

Thomas Smallwood, the baker at Cross Hall, had a brick oven, while up the village street Mrs. Groom had a “brick and pantiled bake-house with steam pipe oven, built in glazed brick.” A gas supply was laid on to her house, and to a few others including Cross House, the Five Bells and Stone House, the foursquare mid-Victorian dwelling built by the Rock family for their own occupation, at the end of their row of smaller dwellings called Rock’s Cottages.

Moving now to the east of the main village area, only part of the hamlet of Well Hill was then in Chelsfield parish, as the district came largely within Shoreham and Lullingstone. In extensive changes made by the Church Commissioners in 1938, the whole of Well Hill was transferred to Chelsfield ecclesiastical parish, but in 1914 the boundary crossed the road just above the Rock and Fountain, then cut behind the cottages facing Back Hill and actually passed through one of them before following the trackway up in front of the Kent Hounds and then turning west to include the Black Cottages. In 1887, to commemorate Queen Victoria’s Golden Jubilee, mains water was laid on between Orpington and Chelsfield, but it is clear that this boon did not extend as far as Well Hill.

Here, although the population was very small, there were two Beerhouses, neither of which had much in the way of basic facilities. The Rock and Fountain, part of the Waring estate, is described as "old, moderate repair, damp... cesspool sewage, water to be carried from pump at Well Hill". At the Kent Hounds, where the owner was C.N. Kidd of Dartford and the landlord was Frank Winchcombe, "pump water" was also relied on. Ground floor plans of the two Beerhouses are included, showing that, in common with many licensed premises of the period, both had Club Rooms. There is no mention of a gas supply in any of the Well Hill properties, so that throughout the area lighting would still have been by candles or oil lamps.

The surveyor noted that a pair of cottages near the Kent Hounds, built of brick, flint, tiles and thatch, were very old and in bad repair; water had to be carried from the adjoining wood and there was simply "no drainage." The tenants, John French and William Baker, paid three shillings a week, as did the occupiers of the Black Cottages nearby – but they at least had cesspools. The pairs of two-bedroom cottages in Back Hill were all said to be in good or moderate repair, and the tenants, including Walter Stone, Henry Blundell and Jane Hatherill, would seem to have had a better bargain, paying only 2s.6d. a week - indeed Rosa Gissing, an old tenant, paid 2s.

Wandering over the boundary into Shoreham parish, there is an unusually flowery description of the most prominent building in the area, Well Hill House. It must have been expensively built, as it is noted that the then owner paid £950 for it in about 1900; the tenant was Mr. H. Lambert. The surveyor reported – "exceptionally good site as regards extensive views, but isolated. Second floor turret - it is alleged that St. Paul's and Westminster may be seen from this room..."

Much of Well Hill which was in Shoreham and Lullingstone parishes was part of the Hart Dyke estate, whose owner at the time of the Valuation Office survey was Sir William Hart Dyke of Lullingstone Castle. The family fortunes had been in steep decline from the time that he had succeeded to the title in 1875[2]. Sir William however was a generous landlord of the old school, and land at Well Hill was let to a number of enterprising fruit farmers, prominent among whom were members of the Foreman, Crowhurst and Hatherill families. The land was productive and the railway stations at Swanley Junction, Knockholt and Chelsfield were within a reasonable distance. In 1893 Sir William had presented the land on which the Mission Church was built, a charming building which still flourishes, and is held in much affection.

The Field Books show that Robert Foreman rented West Wood and almost 30 acres of land in Shoreham on a lease dating from 1900, at a rent of £120 per annum, growing strawberries and bush fruit as well as apples. Living conditions were primitive by modern standards, and the Foreman dwelling was described as "fairly good weatherboard and slate bungalow cottage of 5 rooms and scullery." Such single storey weatherboarded cottages, built from the 1870s onwards, were typical buildings provided by the Lullingstone Estate at Well Hill; only one has survived to this day, incorporated into a modern house.

In the hamlet of Maypole down the hill, everyone enjoyed running water, and a number of different owners are to be found. Hereditaments numbers 149 and 150 are the Blundell property, celebrated through the racy recollections of Derek Sheffield. The survey shows that the property, then owned by John Blundell of 106 Park Street, London W., was let in two parts, described as "pair of weatherboarded, partly brick and tiled roof cottages, very old structure, fair repair." William Packham was the tenant of the larger part, consisting of "first floor 2 bedrooms (one over no. 150) ground floor kitchen, scullery, earth closet, shed," and he also had the whole of the large rear garden. No 150 (tenant Frederick Pursey) has the description "two rooms on ground floor, shed, earth closet." The orchard next door, site of the former parish poorhouse, was part of the Waring estate but was let to T. Blundell.

Because the survey took so long, new properties sometimes had to be added to the maps, and at Maypole there was a notable addition, Hollycroft, the house built for "Willy" Fox and his sister Catherine to live in after he retired from farming Lilleys in 1912. It would seem to have had all the up-to-date features then available, including the unusual luxury for rural areas of "bathroom and WC (Hot and Cold)."

Behind the Blundell cottage, the Black Cottages in Hollybush

Lane are so called because, like those at Well Hill, their weatherboarding was painted black. They belonged to Percival Bowen, farmer, timber merchant, devoted Methodist and Parish Councillor, who lived at Wheatsheaf Farm. He had built the two terraces for his employees in 1898[3], on the site of some very ancient buildings, and they were obviously superior in facilities to many of the older properties. Some if not all had three bedrooms, each cottage being let at the comparatively high rent of 5s. weekly.

There had been much other building activity at Maypole in the 1890s. Miss Sophia Harris had inherited a block of land to the east, where old property which had become ruinous had been demolished, and two pairs of cottages and one detached house had been built instead, let on 99 year leases from 1897. The Harris family also owned the White Hart at Bopeep, on which the Dartford Brewery Company held a lease, then about to expire, and John Charman was the landlord. Fortunately here too a ground floor plan was drawn by the surveyor, particularly interesting as the building has since been so much extended. Even in 1914 it was rather sprawling, and there were two single storey Club Rooms, but most of the building was described as being in bad repair.

Close to Bopeep is one of the ancient farmhouses, Hewitts, which belonged to Arthur Waring. The house itself was occupied by Mrs. Mason, while the 356 acres of agricultural land was let to Alfred May on a 21 year lease from Michaelmas 1893, at £310 per annum. The object of the Valuation Office's exercise being to spy out land which might become valuable for commercial development, the description emphasises that there are good frontages on main roads.

There had been two highly contrasting developments in the far north of the parish. As recounted in another chapter, Alexander Miller-Hallett had come to own Goddington in 1892, and had embarked on an ambitious programme of improvement. However, contrasting with this immaculately kept property, the Craven Estate which bordered it to the east had been laid out from the mid nineties onwards by the architect William Albert Williams, ARIBA, who later developed the Tower Road district in Orpington and lived in a house there called Copper Beeches.

The Craven Estate, which was partly in Orpington and partly in Chelsfield, had evidently not been a successful venture. Mr. Williams had split up the land in Chelsfield Lane into many building plots but by the time of the Valuation Office survey very few houses had been built. The only one in Chelsfield parish nestled close to the boundary with Goddington Park, something which cannot have pleased Mr. Miller-Hallett, while the building itself does not sound at all attractive. The surveyor valued the structure at only £60, and described it as "detached, brick foundation, galvanised and timber 3 roomed bungalow...road roughly formed, not sewered. Bungalow has been apparently empty some time and is in poor repair." In the twenties and thirties more substantial houses began to be built, some on large plots, and it is clear from talking to old inhabitants that it was an idyllic, rural environment in which to grow up at that time.

Green Street Green

This hamlet was partly in Farnborough and partly in Chelsfield, the parish boundary going down the middle of the main road from Orpington to Sevenoaks. At the time of the Tithe Map survey of 1838 there were very few dwellings on the Chelsfield side, only a small cluster of houses, and the Queen's Head, along the main road by the bottom of Worlds End Lane, and some scattered farmhouses. Of these, both Picketts or Lower Green Farm, near Warren Road, and Simmons Haw, a little way up Worlds End Lane, have long since vanished.

The Farrant family of Norstead had owned a good deal of land in Chelsfield from the late eighteenth century onwards, including some 166 acres at or near Green Street Green, and it was with the sale of this in 1887 that Green Street Green began to be opened up for development. This sale of what was then christened the Glentrammon Estate was followed by that of Picketts and 44 acres in 1895, acquired by George Osgood of Pratts Bottom, whose main occupation was coachbuilding. This meant that practically the whole of the district as far as the farmlands of Chelsfield Hall was now open for development.

Mr. Osgood had ambitious plans for what he called the Chelsfield Park Estate, and the Valuation Office maps show it laid out in about 150 plots along the south side of Warren Road

– although I suspect that in most cases these existed on paper only. With some pride he called the central road Osgood Avenue, and other roads were named Avebury Road and Grand View Road. One large central plot was reserved as a "proposed church site," but by 1914 only a few houses had been built, largely in Warren Road.

Elsewhere in Green Street Green there was clearly a demand for modest-sized dwellings, many of which were originally built to house the numerous workers of Fox's Brewery, an important local employer on the Farnborough side of the main road. Kingsley Road and Holly, Beech,Oak, Elm and Ash Roads were laid out off Worlds End Lane, and Laxey and Lezayre Roads off the main road, while more expensive houses were gradually being built in Glentrammon Road. The name of James Dowler, a sand merchant and developer, who was elected as a member of the first Chelsfield Parish Council in 1894, is immortalised in the grandly-named Dowlerville Road.

The title deeds of Fox's Brewery[4] show the reckless way in which the Fox family had borrowed large sums on the security of the Brewery, and matters came to a head when the business was forced to close in 1909. This disaster for the neighbourhood is reflected in the Field Books where in 1910 the surveyor noted about a vacant plot in Glentrammon Road – "building operations are practically at a standstill in this locality owing to the shutting down of the Brewery."

The Baptist church, a prominent building at the foot of Worlds End Lane, had been built in 1906 and could accommodate 230 worshippers. The valuation of the building was a substantial £2500, and the survey mentions the stone tower, tiled Baptistery and piped heating, and also the galvanised iron school adjoining, heated by gas radiator. The Church of England presence at that time was much more modest; St. Mary's Mission church, an offshoot of St. Martin's, noted as having been built in 1907-8, could seat only 75 and was intended as a temporary measure. In the event the permanent church was not consecrated until 1937, and the parish of St. Mary's, which includes Pratts Bottom, was carved out of Chelsfield, Cudham, Farnborough and Orpington in the great ecclesiastical re-arrangements of the following year.[5]

As to the older houses still surviving in Green Street Green just before the Great War, the farmhouse of the former Green Farm was described as dilapidated, and the residual 3 acres of land attached to it were used as a chicken run. Further down the Sevenoaks Road, just beyond the bottom of Worlds End Lane, there still existed what had once been a fine example of a Kentish "yeoman's house," which had fallen on hard times, had been sub-divided and was described in June 1914 as "four timber, partly cement-rendered and tiled cottages ...condemned, very bad repair." Ironically, a photograph of them as picturesque attractions had appeared a little earlier in a guide to Orpington and neighbourhood got up by a local developer.

Close by, the house called Wellhurst, which had formerly been tenanted by Augustine Giles, a Manager at the Brewery, still belonged to Thomas Hamilton Fox, but the premises were used as tea rooms – a sensible development, as Green Street Green was a great venue for cyclists exploring the countryside within easy reach of London. The only farm still functioning was the ancient Chelsfield Hall, which was a dairy farm owned by A.C. Norman, one of the Bromley Common family. The surveyor noted ominously that its 105 acres adjoined the building area at Green Street Green, with good building frontages on the London and Sevenoaks Road and Worlds End Lane. It is quite surprising that, despite the temptations of development, particularly in the inter-War years, the fine old house has survived, and most of the land has remained open to this day.

The Queen's Head at the foot of Worlds End Lane has a long history, but the survey notes that it had been rebuilt in about 1900, with all modern conveniences. The property then belonged to Nalder and Collyer's Brewery and in 1914 J.P. Lord had recently taken over from Henry Bassett as landlord. The property then included the adjoining 3 acre field, now part of Vine Road School grounds, and there was a brick and tile coach house with 6 stalls, and a stable with loft over it.

Pratts Bottom and the far South of the parish

Pratts Bottom was a busy hamlet when it stood on the old coach road, and the building of the new turnpike road over Polhill in the 1830s must have been a severe blow. The hamlet's fortunes revived a little when the railway came, and Chelsfield and Knockholt (originally Halstead) stations were opened in 1868 and 1876 respectively. An alternative form of employment had now become available to farm labourers, and the late Victorian Census returns show that numbers of railway workers had come to live at Pratts Bottom.

The new houses were a little way from the Green, the old centre of the hamlet, and had been built in the angle of the Sevenoaks and Knockholt roads. They consisted of pairs or terraces – Myrtle, Fairlawne and Prospect Cottages, West View and Ethel Terrace – together with the Post Office and Chelsfield's only manufacturing business, a carriage works.

Myrtle Cottages were owned by William Jessup, who lived at Sydenham, and they were perhaps the first of the new development (the surveyor describes them as "old, moderate repair"), being built partly of the traditional flint, partly of brick. They had two bedrooms, gas and running water, and the rent was 4s.3d. weekly. The eight houses in Ethel Terrace of about 1899 were definitely superior, and in very good repair. They each had a parlour with bay window, kitchen, scullery with copper, running water and gas. The rent of five shillings weekly reflects the fairly unusual luxury for a working class home of a third bedroom. By contrast, the former tollgate cottage was still in existence, in the opposite angle of the Sevenoaks and Knockholt roads, and was described as "a very old dilapidated Bungalow, brick and slated, 4 rooms, earth closet" - but the weekly rent was still five shillings.

The carriage works mentioned above belonged to George Osgood, already encountered in his capacity as a developer at Green Street Green. He was in a substantial way of business, the premises, built in about 1887, including two paint shops, a carpenter's shop, a warehouse and store shed. Mr. Osgood also owned and lived in the Post Office building next door.

The Bull's Head, fronting the Green further up Rushmore Hill, then belonged to the brewers Noakes and Co. Ltd. The surveyor estimated that it dated from the early nineteenth century, the heyday of coach travel, although of course there had been an inn on the site for centuries before that. Part of the Halstead Place estate came into Chelsfield, and among its properties were Homewood Cottages, a row of 8 clapboard cottages of a type then common in the district. They had been built in about 1870, and in 1914 they were each let for three shillings weekly; they had two bedrooms but there was only one water tap shared between all the tenants.

Many years ago I wrote a study of the way in which the Commons (or Manorial Waste) at Pratts Bottom and Green Street Green had been encroached upon[6] and I find this a fascinating topic. One of the properties which had been built on the Waste by leave of the Lord of the Manor was a cottage at the junction of the Green and Norstead Lane. It has since been rebuilt, but at the time of the New Domesday survey the primitive original building survived, described as being of brick and flint construction, relying on rain water and being in bad repair. It consisted only of a sitting room and kitchen with scullery downstairs, and one bedroom upstairs.

Opposite it were two houses and shops, then a row of three cottages and gardens known as Walton's Cottages, next to the forge and bakehouse; all this property was owned by D.W. Walton. He lived at the smithy, which had two fires, and the brick, flint and galvanised bakehouse had one oven.

Southwards from Pratts Bottom itself the land continues to rise, and the parish gradually narrows; there were a number of scattered farmhouses and cottages, but in general the area was pasture and woodland. When Black's Guide a little earlier had called it "wild, romantic and sequestered as the backwoods of America" that was not so very far from the truth.

As described in the chapter on the Manor of Norstead, in 1909 the wealthy businessman A.W. Machonochie had begun to acquire much of the estate in Chelsfield, Cudham and Knockholt which had belonged to the Earl of Derby. This included Cacketts Farm and New Year's Cottage which, although much closer to Cudham village than Chelsfield, were nevertheless in the latter parish.

The present house at Cacketts replaces the old farmhouse which, as mentioned in the survey dated April 1912, had been destroyed by fire, evidently not long before. The house and over 166 acres let with it were occupied by S.M. Dennis, who ran it as a stud farm; the complex of buildings included electricity plant and an engine house, while a quadrangle of brick stabling with 14 loose boxes was in the course of erection[7].

The Gamekeeper by Leslie Collins

The farmhouse is a fine building, standing well on a hilltop and looking not unlike a miniature French chateau, a lasting memorial to Mr. Machonochie's wealth and taste.

Not far away, down narrow roads which are still unfrequented, lies another of his buildings, New Year's Cottage, about which the surveyor noted "the original cottage has been pulled down and since April 1909 a substantial brick built and slate bungalow erected as a shooting box and cottage for gamekeeper..." and it must surely have been designed by the same architect as Cacketts. £1000 had been expended on the rebuilding, and £280 on connecting it to a water supply – very large sums in 1912. There were substantial outbuildings, including "large game larder, Large Motor House, Dog Kennels etc.," and the description conjures up vivid pictures of Mr. Machonochie's business associates motoring down from town for weekend shooting parties in the days just before the Great War.

References

1 The Valuation Books are at Bromley Local Studies Library, reference 687/6/2-3. The maps and Field Books are at the PRO, references respectively IR121/5/95-100, 107, 110-111 and IR58/14220-6.

2 See "Lullingstone Park" by Susan Pittman (Meresborough Books, 1983) for an excellent history of the Lullingstone estate and its owners.

3 Mrs. Gwen Bowen kindly lent me the papers relating to this rebuilding.

4 CKS, U697/T28.

5 See map at the Church of England Record Office.

6 Typescript and maps in Bromley Local Studies Library.

7 Plans are at Bromley Planning Office, but those for the farmhouse itself are missing.

Chapter 2

SCANDAL IN THE PARISH

"Perhaps their loves, or else their sheep,
Was all that did their silly thoughts so busy keep"
- from Milton's "Ode on the morning of Christ's Nativity."

It is difficult to get beneath the skin of our ancestors and to try to see things as they saw them; generally speaking, one can only guess at the tensions and passions which must have existed beneath the surface in even the best-behaved parishes, but from time to time evidence of these emerges. I have put together here some of the events which surfaced in documents relating to Chelsfield in the sixteenth century.

Little is known of most of the pre-Reformation clergy who served Chelsfield as Rectors or assistant priests, although the names of some are familiar through being mentioned in wills. One such is John Williams, who figures in the lengthy will[1] of Alice Bray widow, who died in 1510; her portrait in brass is still to be seen on the chancel floor. She was the sister of the previous Rector, Richard Bonaventure, and it is clear from the detailed provisions she made that she had given much thought to her funeral arrangements, and to the provision of requiem masses for the good of her soul and those of her family. She was a lady of some wealth, and among her bequests she left her great cauldron of 50 gallons and her lesser maser of 2 gallons with a silver and gilt band to "John Williams, now parson of Chelsfield," who evidently stood well in her favour.

Not very long after this, on 8 November 1512, allegations about this same priest were being recorded in the Act Book of the Consistory Court of Rochester[2], at a session held in Deptford parish church. The survival of the depositions made by numerous witnesses from Chelsfield, reported verbatim, is a fortunate chance which enables us to catch the nuances of their speech. Initially, the allegations made seem on the face of it to be rather petty, for example Richard Wales' deposition just to the effect that the Rector was often seen with one Alice Reyman. Richard Colgate built on this and added that these two frequently conversed in the Rectory, and that many people talked of it, even as far as Cray and Shoreham, and their behaviour was damaging the reputation of the whole parish. Richard added that people from other parishes said "Ye be to blame for your parson and Alice Rayman to suffer them as ye doo for because ye leye no watche for them in ther suspiciose commyng to gidder" [that is, their suspicious coming together].

Things began to warm up a good deal when Richard Letcote enlarged on the theme that Chelsfield was being laughed at by other parishes and said that men in Shoreham, Eynsford and Cudham talked of the matter and said "All your parish ar bawdes for to the parson and Alice Reyman and Meller wif for there drawyng so to gidder." Robert Nichols said it was " the common fame" that not only were Alice Reyman and the Rector often suspiciously together, but that Meller's wife also went with him, adding that she was not content with Alice Reyman's conversation and liked that of the Rector. The most memorable deposition, which would undoubtedly hit the headlines even in today's press, is that in which Agnes Nichols, probably Robert's wife, is reported as saying to Alice Reyman, "Thou prestes hore thy husbounde lepte owte of his own chambre wyndow whan the parson of Chellisfielde com in to thy chambre and my husband did never so."

15th C Priest brass, Chelsfield Church

Calling her a priest's whore must have come very high on the list of the most insulting taunts to throw at a woman in pre-Reformation times and Alice Reyman would certainly seem to have been cast as the local bad girl. John Williams was formally charged with adultery with her in December

Young ladies - brass, c.1470

1514, but he must have been exonerated or absolved since his name disappears from the Court records after that, and he continued in office until his death in 1532. However, the case rumbled on and became ever more complex, with allegations of adultery, now involving John Meller and Agnes Nichols. Quite where the truth lay in all this it is now impossible to decide, but so far as the allegations about the Rector are concerned I think it is fair comment to say that the celibate clergy must have been vulnerable to every piece of gossip in the parish, and to every whisper of scandal. There would have been few parishioners with any education, and perhaps "Meller's wife" did simply find the other village women's conversation boring compared to that of the Rector, and Agnes Nichols was just being spiteful in recounting the story about Alice Reyman's husband jumping out of the window when the priest called; we shall never know.

Many of the records of the Diocese of Rochester have been lost, but one fortunate survival is the Archdeacon's Visitation book, covering the period 1587 to 1620[3]. The Visitation articles and injunctions issued by the Archdeacons posed a great many searching questions. Among the topics covered in the articles issued by Elizeus Burgess, Archdeacon of Rochester[4] at a slightly later period, are:

"Whether is there any of your parish that do not come to church at all, or any that do but seldom resort thither (being of the age of 16 years and above)? Whether are there in your parish, any that are known or vehemently suspected to have committed incest, adultery, fornication or other incontinency ...or any blasphemer, common drunkard, swearer, bawd, common scold, common usurer, maker of seditious libels, or any that have fought or brawled in the church or churchyard?

Whether there are any in your parish, that doth use to work upon Sundays and holidays, or open their shops for sale of their wares upon any of these days?"

The Archdeacon held periodic Visitations when the parochial

clergy would present parishioners for any misdemeanours, and would sometimes be presented themselves. The Rev George Smith, the first of the three of that name, was Rector of Chelsfield with the chapelry of Farnborough attached for fifty years, from 1576 to 1626. He was a model parish priest, and his concern for his parish and chapelry is reflected in the Archdeacon's records.

In 1587 there is an entry (in fact under Farnborough) which refers to "one Agnes Larke... which hath had two children begotten and borne in adulterie and now as she her selfe sayeth is with Child againe by one Richard Netlingham of Chelsfeilde which is the thirde tyme that she hathe thus used her selfe..." The baptisms of Denise and William, two illegitimate children of "Agnes Lark, singlewoman" are recorded in Chelsfield registers in 1580 and 1583, while the enigmatically named Fortune, no doubt the subject of the presentment, was baptised at Farnborough in 1587/8. It seems that her parentage was generally accepted, since in the register entry of her burial in 1601 she is described as "Fortune (as yt ys thought) Netlingham." Similarly, when her half sister Denise was married in 1610 her father's surname (otherwise unknown) is broadly hinted at, the register describing her as "Dionisia Lark alias Margerram." Meanwhile, Agnes herself had at last settled down and had married John Dyer at Chelsfield in 1590.

The Larke family seem to have been unpopular with the Rector, for in 1587 Thomas Larke of Farnborough is presented "for that he seldome is or never cometh to Churche nor his Chyldren he hathe a very wicked householde." Thomas Larke and his wife also appear in the Rochester Act Books, being presented in 1590 for not frequenting their parish church, while Thomas has a separate entry accusing him of being "a Rayler and a bad person." It is not clear if there were any tangible results from all these presentments, but the Larke family, who owned two small holdings, including one known as Larkehouse, did not long continue in the neighbourhood; perhaps they felt unwelcome. The last entry relating to them in the registers of either Chelsfield or Farnborough was in 1610.

Agnes' errant father must have died before 1612, as the

Chelsfield Manor Rental for that year gives the owners of Larke House - one tenement and orchard at Green Street Green in Chelsfield held by annual Quitrent of twopence halfpenny - as " the heirs of Thomas Larke." In deeds of 1623[5], Edward and William Larke disposed of their properties in Chelsfield and Farnborough "formerly of Thomas Larke and James Larke," Edward then being described as a labourer of Coventry, Warwicks. and William as a shoemaker of Badby, Northants. When Edward's property was sold on soon afterwards there was a clause in the conveyance which may perhaps be an oblique reference to problems experienced in dealing with the rather slapdash Larke family. The vendor, Francis Packman, promised the purchaser, James Stiles, that he would hand over to him all such "deedes Evidences Muniments and wrightings whatsoever ...consarninge anie now or heretofore the lands of the Larkes or anie parte or parcell thereof" as he might "lawfullye gett and obtaine without suit or trouble of lawe..."

The feeling that offenders disgraced the whole parish, which shows up so strongly in the case about John Williams and others, persisted well beyond the Reformation, and is demonstrated in another presentation to the Archdeacon, in May 1588. William Colgatte and Elizabeth, wife of John Letcott, were presented "for accompanying together at sundry suspicious times and places to the slander of our parish and dishonour of God, notwithstanding that they have been often rebuked therefore." At the same Visitation, held in Deptford church, Thomas Byrlinge and Emma Fletcher of Chelsfield were presented "for keeping company in their houses and selling victuals on the sabbath days and festival days in time of divine service namely the 28 of April last at evening prayer time."

1588 was a lawless year at Chelsfield, where in yet another case William Brasier, John Pratt senior, Richard Kingslande and John Eve were presented "for abusing some part of the sabbath contrary to God's laws and the Queen's as namely the Sunday next before Easter ..." Somewhat unusually, there is a note of the response made by the accused but the writing, always difficult in this type of record, is partly illegible at that point, although it would seem that the reply refers to the accused only having undertaken urgent and necessary work on the land on the Sabbath.

Turning from ecclesiastical to lay jurisdiction, it is always satisfying to find an incident in one source amplified in another. In the burial register of Chelsfield appears under 5 June 1570: Simon de Shartresse a frenchman killed at Rishmore hill. This intriguing entry is amplified in the records of Canterbury Assizes[6], where on 11 July 1570 Thomas Stubberfield and John Hall, yeomen of Chevening, were indicted for felonious killing. It was noted that by an inquisition held at Chelsfield on 12 June 1570 on the body of Simon Deshartresse, a jury found that on the night of 10 June, Deshartresse was travelling along a road at Chelsfield in company with John Frett and Bartholomew Martyn, merchant strangers of London, when they met Stubberfield and Hall. A quarrel broke out and in the course of it Stubberfield and Hall attacked Deshartresse at a place called "Nocholes" [?Knockholt]. Stubberfield struck him with a cudgel (value 2d.) and Hall with a sword (value 20d.), killing him. Arthur Grene of Chipstead yeoman is indicted as an accessory. Stubberfield and Hall were found guilty, but "allowed clergy"; Grene was found not guilty.

As will be seen, the dates in the two records do not agree with each other, but this detail apart, I wonder where the truth of the matter lay - was it just another case of heaving half a brick at a stranger, or was there perhaps some deeper motive?

<u>References</u>

[1] CKS, Rochester Consistory DRb/PWr6.

[2] CKS, DRb/Pa5.

[3] CKS, Dra/Vb5.

[4] See "Visitation articles and injunctions of the early Stuart Church" edited by Kenneth Fincham, published by the Church of England Record Society, 1998, vol. II pages 75-79.

[5] Harris MSS A5-7.

[6] See "Kent Indictments Elizabeth I" edited by Professor J.S. Cockburn, PRO publication 1979, entry 531.

Chapter 3

AT THE WORLD'S END

" My messuage or tenement commonly called or known by the name of the Worlds End..."

- from the will and testament of Thomas Mace, husbandman, 1730.

This is the first reference I have found to the curious name Worlds End. On consulting John Field's authoritative work "English field names" published by Alan Sutton in 1989 I found that he refers to a number of parishes where "The World's End" and variations occur. He gives the derivation as "land on or near the boundary of the parish," and although, strictly, this does not apply at Chelsfield, this small farm was certainly well away from the village, and also some distance from the settlements of Green Street Green and Pratts Bottom. Incidentally the road we know today as World's End Lane was called Big Lane on an estate map of 1774, photographed by Arthur Waring.

In the records of the Manor of Chelsfield Worlds End was known as Newfield, and as these kept strictly to the traditional descriptions it was not until 1803[1] that the new name is mentioned even in passing. It paid to the Lord of the Manor a Quitrent of 1s.4d. per annum, which was typical for a small farm with a few acres of land attached. The history of both owners and occupiers may be traced from the manorial documents, starting with the Rental of 1612, when Thomas Cox held "a tenement and lands in Chelsfield called Newefield late Jetors." The Jetor or Jetour family had been important people in the parish from at least the fifteenth century, but they had died out. However, at least a dim memory of them survived, because as late as 1844 "Geeters Crofte" is given as the "ancient name" of three fields near the church, in the schedule of demesne lands of the Manor[2].

Newfield went from the Cox family to William Chapman who in 1690 left it[3] to his son Thomas. He by 1717 had sold it to the Thomas Mace from whose will[4] I have quoted above. Although he only called himself a husbandman, in fact he was quite prosperous, and could perhaps have qualified for the higher rank of yeoman, since he owned not only Newfield or Worlds End but also a cottage called Chalkhole House (just to the south of the present Chalkhole Cottages at Maypole) and a small field nearby called Breach Croft. Thomas evidently died childless, and in quite a complicated will he left the three holdings to his three sisters, with remainder to their specified children.

Worlds End went to his sister Jane Wakeling for life, then at her death to her son John Wakeling, who was a Bromley shopkeeper – although no doubt related to the Wakelen or Wakelyn family who, like the Maces, had lived for generations in Chelsfield. According to the manorial documents he too died childless and the farm went to his sister's husband John May. By 1799, the property had been sold to John Hills, and with him we begin to be on firmer ground.

The story of the Hills family is one of great worldly success. John Hills' entry into the parish was beset with problems, when he was called up before the Magistrates[5] to prove that he was legally entitled to settlement in the parish. The record reads – "2 April 1781: John Hills now residing in Chelsfield, labourer, states that in 1779 he held and rented a house in Chelsfield at £6.6s.0d. per annum, which he held for a whole year. He was married at Chelsfield to Mary late Trull and they have one child, Mary, 2." On this evidence, showing that he was a man of some little substance and unlikely to become a charge on the Parish, he was adjudged to be legally settled in Chelsfield. This was a matter of vital importance to him and his family, as otherwise they could have been forcibly returned to the parish in which he could be proved to have a legal settlement.

By some means which I have not yet discovered, they became substantial and well-respected inhabitants. John Hills died in 1829, and his son William in 1868, in possession not only of Worlds End but of other properties in Chelsfield. His will was proved at "under £25,000" – a surprisingly large amount, particularly for one whose father had been regarded suspiciously as a potential pauper.

Because William Hills' will is exceptionally detailed and mentions so many of his relations to whom he left generous bequests, it has been possible with much help from my son Matthew Copus to compile an enormously large family tree. A copy of this has been deposited at Bromley Local Studies Library, together with more detailed notes on Worlds End. William left many bequests to the grandchildren of his aunt Elizabeth Rawlings, among whom he particularly favoured David Stanley of Marden, farmer. He was left not only £1000 3% annuities but also "the two cottages and barn and 7 acres of plantation ground known as Worlds End, now in my own occupation." In an unusual gesture, he left £5 to every widow and widower who had lived in Chelsfield for at least 5 years.

David lost no time in taking possession, and in the Maidstone Journal of October 1868, when he was living at Tan House, Marden, he advertised for a tenant for his "small farm... known as the World's End." His full name was David Shaw Stanley, and by the time of the 1891 Census he had retired to Chelsfield, where he was living as a boarder with Mary Morgan – another beneficiary of William Hills' will – at Cross House in Chelsfield village, aged 81, a widower "living on own means."

David too died childless, and his will proved in 1896 is another treasure-house of information for the family historian, mirroring that of William Hills, with bequests to a wide range of relatives. He left half of his Chelsfield property for life to his nephew, also called David Shaw Stanley, with remainder to his children. The other half was left to another nephew on similar terms, but it was David who is given as the sole owner in the Valuation Office records of 1914[6]; he first appears in Kelly's Directory of 1911, when he had evidently decided to live at Worlds End himself. The old farmhouse had been let as two cottages for many years, but he converted it back into a single house.

The surveyor's report in the Field Book describes the property as "a pair of red brick and tiled cottages. Old structure and repair (now thrown into one residence). 2 sitting rooms: 2 scullery: kitchen and 3 bedrooms. Orchard land. Old fruit trees: principally damson: some apple trees: under fruit (Mr. Stanley is now in residence and is gradually grubbing the land). Weather boarded and pantiled barn and stable: coach-house, 2 earth closets, no water except rain water."

Mr. Stanley also rented land in the village - Bellropes Field and, adjoining it, the western end of East field, on part of which the Village Hall now stands. The land was described in the Valuation Office records as a market garden, where apples and raspberries were grown; there were also worksheds and a decayed stable.

Worlds End Farm was left as a little rural backwater surrounded by new houses after Gillmans (or Julian) Brimstone Farm was sold for development in 1920, but Mr. Stanley continued to operate it as a smallholding. When I read "Time remembered," a charming and accurately-recalled book of reminiscences by "Miss Read" (Dora Saint)[7] about her childhood in Chelsfield in the twenties, I was interested to find a reference to Mr. Stanley. Mrs. Saint's family lived in one of the new houses on Chelsfield Hill, but she went to Chelsfield school and also had music lessons from Miss Hill, who lived at Mount Hall. One winter's day the snow had begun to fall while her lesson was in progress, and Mr. Stanley (who delivered milk in the district) gave her a lift home in his milk float, a blissful journey through the flurry of snow which she thought the most exciting ride she had ever had. When I wrote to Mrs. Saint about this and other episodes in her book I had a kind response in which she said that Mr. Stanley was a charming man – "I'm sorry his house has gone" she added, for that was indeed the fate which had overtaken the ancient Worlds End farmhouse.

It was perhaps surprising that it had lasted as long as it did, given the development value of the seven acres attached to it. Standing rather in the path of possible access, the farmhouse was demolished in 1962; fortunately the indefatigable Derek Stoyel of Orpington was at hand to record its appearance before the bulldozers moved in.

References

[1] CKS, U55/M393.
[2] Waring MSS
[3] CKS, Rochester Consistory DRb/PW37.
[4] PCC PROB 11/647
[5] Bromley Settlement examinations, indexed by Elizabeth Silverthorne and published by the North West Kent Family History Society
[6] PRO, Field Book IR58/14220 nos. 87/88/89/90.
[7] First published by Michael Joseph Ltd. in 1986

Chapter 4

CHURCH, PRIEST AND PEOPLE BEFORE THE REFORMATION

"I leave to the high altar of Chelsfield for tithes negligently forgotten twelve pence."

-a bequest found in many pre-Reformation wills.

On 25 May 1895 the Lewisham Antiquarian Society visited Chelsfield church under the guidance of their secretary, Leland L.Duncan F.S.A., a noted antiquary. Duncan, a Civil Servant, who was a friend of the Rector, the Rev. Henry Broughton Barnes, certainly knew his subject extremely well. It was he who through his researches established beyond doubt that the dedication of the church is in honour of St. Martin. I find it endearing that he worked on mediaeval wills, then housed at Somerset House, during his lunchtime, and occasionally his transcriptions of those of Chelsfield people appeared in the Parish Magazine[1] .

The lecture which Mr. Duncan gave on the occasion of the visit to the church also appeared in the Parish Magazine, and on reading it one is transported back to a different world. His scholarly, precise, somewhat pedantic tones come over very clearly:

"I may commence by reminding you that we are some 450 feet above the level of the sea, in a spur of the range of hills forming the North Downs. Chelsfield Church is thus a prominent object for many miles, and I daresay its steeple is known by sight at any rate, to many who have never ventured up the hillside from Orpington...

When the returns, from which the Domesday Book was compiled, were sent in, many of them contained two words which perhaps convey more to us at the present day than anything else in the various entries – "Ibi ecclesia" – "Here is a

Church." Now although several places round us are stated to have possessed a Church those responsible for the returns relating to Chelsfield did not think it a part of their duty (as in truth it was not) to make any statement on that point. If, however, there was no Church here in 1084 one was very soon afterwards built, and the nave walls of the present building date from that time. You will see two little Norman windows yet remaining."

Dorothy Cox in her popular "Book of Orpington" erroneously states that Chelsfield church "is mentioned in Domesday," and also cites the discovery of earlier foundations when the vestry was being built in 1893 as evidence of the existence of a previous building "which may have been built many years before the Norman Conquest." This is inaccurate; certainly there had been a building on approximately the site of the present vestry, but it had been a later addition to the existing Norman church.

Having said this, there is undoubtedly sound evidence for there having been a church at Chelsfield in Saxon times. Dr. Gordon Ward in Archaeologia Cantiana volume XLIV (1932) wrote a paper on a very early record of parish churches and chapelries listed in the Textus Roffensis, in Rochester Cathedral Library. A translation of its title given by Dr. Ward is - "concerning the number of churches of the bishopric of Rochester and the payments which they each make when they receive the holy chrism [oil] from the episcopal mother church." Although the list appears in the Textus itself in about 1115, the question of its actual date has been argued over by scholars. Dr. Ward was inclined to the view that it is a copy of a document dating from not later than 1089, that is, very soon after the completion of the Domesday Book.

Chelsfield (written Cilesfeld) appears in the Textus Roffensis list, with the chapelry of Farnborough (Faernberga) even then attached to it. Rather provocatively, Dr. Ward entitled his paper "Saxon churches in the Textus Roffensis." He argued persuasively that it was unlikely that all 152 of the churches and chapels mentioned would have been built in the years between 1066 and 1089 and that the great majority of them would therefore have been in existence in Saxon times. F.C. Elliston Erwood F.S.A., another eminent authority, later agreed with this view and wrote[2] that inclusion in the Textus Roffensis list is "generally accepted as a proof of pre-conquest origin." To sum up, therefore, it may be stated that, despite there being no reference to Chelsfield church in Domesday Book, the available evidence points to the existence of a Saxon building.

The chancel and the eastern part of the nave date from about 1080 to 1100; John Newman points out[3] that soon afterwards the nave was greatly lengthened. In the thirteenth century the east wall of the chancel was rebuilt, pierced by attractive lancets in the new pointed style, and it may have been at this period too that the chapel mentioned above was added to the north. The tower to the north of the nave and St. John's chapel to the south also date from the thirteenth century, while the porch is fourteenth century. At least 450 years elapsed between the building of the present church and the Reformation, and some 450 years have passed since then. Although the present appearance of the interior is very different to that of say 1530, there had been changes in liturgy and practice in the centuries before that, which contributed to the way the interior appeared just before the Reformation. It is fortunate that the wills of many inhabitants are in existence[4], and the wording of their pious bequests enables us to build up a vivid picture of the church before most of the decoration and fittings were swept away in the changes of the mid sixteenth century.

Very few wills have survived from before 1383, but registers recording those of a few prominent people were, and still are, kept at Lambeth Palace, and so escaped the flames of the Peasants' Revolt, which consumed the rest. Among the Lambeth wills appears a familiar name, that of Sir Otho de Grandison, Lord of the Manor of Chelsfield, who died in 1358. Although he was a powerful landowner, and the family "power base" was in Devon, where his brother John was Bishop of Exeter, he was obviously very attached to Chelsfield. On the face of it this is surprising, as it must have been distinctly bleak here in the fourteenth century, and so far as I am aware there was never any large fortified Manor house, such as would appeal to a tough old soldier.

Sir Otho's will[5] is very detailed in the provisions for his funeral, and for masses to be said for the good of his soul and those of his relatives and friends. Extracts from the will are worth quoting at some length, translated from the original Latin –

"My body to be buried in the church of the College of St. Mary de Ottery in the Diocese of Exeter if I happen to die there, or if I happen to die at Chelsfield then I leave my body to be buried in the chapel of St. John of Chelsfield, beseeching and supplicating my friends and executors of their love that they will not permit any armed man or horse to go before my body on the day of my burial nor my corpse to be covered with any coloured or golden cloth or with any arms but only a white cloth marked with a red cross ...I leave to the high altar of the church of Chelsfield for tithes forgotten 20s.

I leave for the sustenation of two wax tapers of 18 lb [the equivalent of nearly 200 modern household candles] to be lighted every day for ever at the Elevation of the Sacrament in the church of Chelsfield four good cows and twenty good mother sheep together with the wax left on the day of my death. To the light of Blessed Mary in the church of Chelsfield two good cows. I leave for the sustenation of a wax taper of 3 lb. for ever burning on solemn days to the left of the light of Blessed Mary in the said church 20s. I leave to the painting of the image of Blessed Mary in the said church 20s. To the sustenation of a great wax taper of 10 lb. for ever burning upon solemn days before the image of Christ in the said church 40 mother sheep with the wax upon the said taper existing on the day of my death... to forty of my poor tenants at Chelsfield 40s. [present day equivalent about £600]. To the maintenance of an honest chaplain to celebrate for my soul the divine offices in the church of Chelsfield for 3 years £15 [now about £4500]. To the work of the church of Chelsfield for the soul of Stephen Pratt 20s. [now about £300]."

In the event, Otho must have died in Devon, because he was buried at Ottery St. Mary and he and his wife lie in the church there beneath elaborate tombs displaying their effigies. At Chelsfield though Otho has not been neglected, and his coat of arms in stained glass was put up in the east window of St. John's chapel after that was restored to its original use in 1950.

In mediaeval times, a common form with which to open a will was "I leave my soul to Almighty God and to our blessed lady Saint Mary and to all the holy company of heaven." Although the wealthy were particularly anxious to ease their passage through the perils of Purgatory, testators in quite humble circumstances would make provision for the good of their souls and those of their friends and families before dealing with more worldly matters. In a bequest typical of many, John Beveryche in 1513[6] provided for "an honest priest to sing for my soul, my wife's soul and all Christian souls in Chelsfield church for one whole year, and for his salary or wages to have £6.13s.4d." Often specific images and other items are mentioned, and a study of the wills enables us to build up a picture of the interior of St. Martin's as it was gradually enriched in the centuries leading up to the Reformation. There have always been fashions in church architecture and furnishings, and these have been followed at Chelsfield as elsewhere, both before and after the Reformation and indeed up to the present day.

The original Norman church would have consisted simply of nave and chancel, and the arch between them was narrow, no more than about ten feet wide[7], and it was also low and had a rounded head. Some of those at mass in the nave, the people's part of the building, might not have not have been able to see very clearly the high point of the service, the elevation of the Host at the High Altar, and their view would have been still further restricted when a rood screen was added.

Rood screens, which came into fashion in England by the end of the thirteenth century, carried a large crucifix (or rood) flanked by figures of Our Lady and St. John. The dramatic effect of such an arrangement may be seen locally at St. Mary's, Kemsing, in a sensitive reconstruction by the architect Sir Ninian Comper.

At Chelsfield, Otho de Grandison's bequest in 1358 to "the image of Christ" may be a reference to the rood, and the screen with the roodloft above was certainly in place at least by 1472, when William Cokke left "to the roodloft 2 bushels of barley." The Rev. Richard Bonaventure or Bounter, the Rector, in his will[8] dated 1493 asked for his body to be buried "in the body of the Church of Chelsfield before the crucifix there or else in any other place or Church to lie before the crucifix where I fortune to die." Evidence that the screen was embellished by lights is provided in another bequest of John Beveryche, who in 1513 left "twenty shillings to buy latten [brass alloy] bowls to stand underneath the tapers that is before the Roodloft."

There are references to quite a number of images of saints, but in most cases one can only guess where they were placed. Duncan states that generally the main image of the Blessed Virgin would stand in the chancel, on a bracket let into the wall on the north side of the high altar, and there is confirmation of this position in two wills. In 1493 Richard Aschlegh left 6s.8d. "to paint the image of the Blessed Mary in the chancel" – our mediaeval ancestors liked their churches to look bright and colourful - while in 1509 Alice Bray wrote of "the image of our Lady in the North part of the church," leaving money to enable a taper to be kept burning before it during High Mass for ever after. She also provided for tapers to be lit similarly before the images of St. Martin and St. James.

The light of St. John, presumably in that chapel, is mentioned in the will of Thomas Jetour senior in 1472, and he also left twelve pence "to painting the image of Our Lady of Pity." This representation of the Blessed Virgin with the figure of the dead Christ is mentioned in the same year by William Cokke, who left a cow "to find a taper before Our Lady of Pity." Finally on the topic of images, Alen Colegate in 1508 left seven shillings to find a taper to burn before the Trinity for evermore.

It was usual for the interior walls of mediaeval churches to be covered in paintings, few of which have survived. By their nature they were vulnerable to damp and decay, and they were also attacked by the sixteenth century reformers who whitewashed them over as being superstitious, so that today not a trace survives at Chelsfield.

On Sundays and major Feast days it was customary for High Mass to be celebrated, probably therefore calling on the services of the priests employed to sing for the souls of the departed in accordance with the provisions of some of the wills mentioned above. All parishioners were expected to hear mass on these occasions, and no doubt the great majority would have done so, although it would have been a long trek from the

An impression of St Martin's church interior circa 1500.
Drawing by John Blundell, 2003.

furthest parts of the parish, which were much closer to Cudham church. The scene would have been one of primitive splendour when, as we have seen, banks of tapers were burning before the images and along the roodloft, while clouds of incense ascended with the prayers of the faithful and must also have helped to mask the stench of unwashed humanity.

In the earlier period at least there would have been no pews, but these gradually began to come into use, at least for the better-off. Present-day stress on the participation of the congregation in the action of the eucharist would have been alien to pre-Reformation ideas. The priest celebrated on behalf of the congregation, who were expected to kneel and pray meekly and quietly on the floor, rising at certain moments such as the reading of the Gospel. Above all, at the consecration and the elevation of the Host they were to kneel with both hands raised in adoration[9].

The clergy would have been among the few who were literate, and in rural parishes they could well have felt isolated, and have lacked intellectual stimulation. In an unusual bequest in the will of Roger Godestre[10] of Chelsfield, proved in 1368, he leaves to his parish church a book of Canon Law for the edification of the clergy and also two other books bound in one cover, consisting of a book of mysteries and a popular "Book of Sentences" which Dr. Paul Lee tells me was a biblical digest. I know nothing of Roger Godestre apart from the indications in his will that he was a devout parishioner. He would seem to have been sympathetic to liturgical trends of his time, because in addition to bequests to different orders of Friars he left forty pence to the parson of Halstead to celebrate "a trentall of masses according to the new mode."

A common feature of mediaeval wills is the sense that things would always go on as they were; the pious testators envisaged that the lighting of the candles for which they had provided would endure "for ever." I wonder if, in practice, even in pre-Reformation times these commemorations were really kept up for very long, particularly if there were no surviving local descendants. Alice Bray makes reference in 1509 to a record which, up to the Reformation, was perhaps a surer guarantee of being remembered, when she asked that "the parson or his deputy ... every Sunday or at such time as he reads Bede Roll shall pray for my soul." The Bede Roll commemorated the more substantial departed parishioners, who in return for a suitable contribution were assured that their names would for ever after be remembered, and Alice left 8d. per annum for this purpose.

Pilgrimages to be undertaken on behalf of the testator appear in three wills. Thomas Fryth (1492) provided for his Executor John Beverege to go on pilgrimage for him to the shrines of Master John Shorn and Our Lady of Crowham, and Martin Jetour (1503) asked that his sister Agnes should go on a pilgrimage for him. John Beveryche (1513) left 13s.4d. to William Clement his Executor "to bere myne offeryng and my wifes offeryng to or Lady of Walsingham."

There are a number of wills in which money is left to enrich the building or to repair the fabric. In 1516 John Cock of Tonbridge, who owned a tenement in Chelsfield, left 40s. to the church, to buy "some ornament such as the parishioners think most needful." William Clement in 1526 left forty pence towards the repair of the bell, which is the first reference to bells that I have found; Robert Mablott in 1479 left chalices price forty shillings each to Chelsfield, Orpington and Farnborough churches.

To quote again from Leland L. Duncan's talk of 1895 – "There was a custom in the marriage service of the bringing in of a cup which was blessed by the priest and partaken of by those present; the custom also obtained at Churchings. John Beveryche in 1513 left 'to the Churche of Chellisfeld a maser cuppe which I bought of Mastresse Alys [most probably Alice Bray] for thys entent that every childewife and also every bride shall drink in it as long as it lastith.' " Alas, neither this nor Robert Mablott's chalice survived the turmoils of the Reformation.

Henry Beverych in 1509 left seven mother sheep to maintain for ever a taper to burn before the Sepulchre until Easter, then to burn before the image of the Holy Trinity. The tomb of Robert de Brun, a Rector who died in 1417, consists of an unusual arched recess in the north wall of the chancel, and it seems possible that this may have been used for the Easter Sepulchre ceremonies. From the number of bequests of sheep and other animals to the church, it appears that Chelsfield maintained a parish flock which would be farmed out. Unfortunately all the early parochial records have long since been lost so it is not possible to discover any details of the way this system worked, or indeed about many other aspects of the history of the parish in mediaeval times.

References

[1] A good run of Parish Magazines is kept in St. Martin's vestry.

[2] Arch. Cant. volume LXV, page 146.

[3] See the Chelsfield entry in "West Kent and the Weald" in the Penguin Buildings of England series.

[4] Unless otherwise stated, the wills quoted are from the probate registers of the Consistory Court of Rochester at CKS, Maidstone, reference DRb/Pwr 3 to 10. I am grateful to Dr. Paul Lee for having provided me with abstracts of these records, adding to the researches of Leland L.Duncan, on which I have also drawn.

[5] Lambeth will 148a Islip.

[6] PCC, PROB 11/17.

[7] CCA, additional MSS 55 - plan and notes by the Rev. Andrew Burnside.

[8] PCC, PROB 11/11.

[9] On this and related topics see "The stripping of the altars" by Eamon Duffy, Yale University Press, 1992.

[10] Lambeth will 120b Langham.

Chapter 5

CHURCH, PRIEST AND PEOPLE AFTER THE REFORMATION

"The Bishop of Rome hath no greater jurisdiction committed to him by God in this realm of England than any other foreign Bishop."

- *Renunciation of the Papal authority by the clergy of West Kent, 1534*

The declaration against the Papal authority was signed on behalf of Chelsfield by Thomas Glayve, the curate, and it marked a significant step in the progress of the Reformation. Over the centuries oceans of ink have been spilled in controversy about the causes, the course and the effects of this movement. My modest aim is to look at some of the ways in which it affected the church and the parish of Chelsfield, and in this I am seriously hampered by the lack of vital documentation such as Churchwardens' accounts, as those for the period before the eighteenth century have long since disappeared.

Despite the element of superstition in later mediaeval devotion, it is impossible to doubt the sincerity of the attachment of Chelsfield people to their church, their traditional religion and the saints before whose images so many tapers were burned. It must have been a bewildering experience for simple parishioners to live through the years of the Reformation, and to witness the wholesale destruction of revered images, of vestments, stained glass and missals, the brief reappearance of the old order under Mary and the final Anglican settlement when Elizabeth succeeded her.

Whatever their true feelings, a very strong motive for acquiescence in these changes would have been self-preservation, and on the side of the reformers there were some powerful local figures, men who had done well out of the rich pickings which were to be had, who therefore had a vested interest in seeing that the new order was firmly established. Percyval Hart of Lullingstone, who had acquired from the Crown the important Manor of Great Orpington and other property after the suppression of the Monastery of Christ Church Canterbury, was one such. He was one of the Commissioners appointed in 1552 to have inventories made, listing what goods remained in each parish church for the decent maintenance of the services. The inventory for Chelsfield[1] shows that, apart from a Bible and a volume of the paraphrases of Erasmus, there were then three bells in the steeple, a handbell, a silver chalice and just one set of vestments, while another chalice, a cope and "one vestment of cloth of tissue" had been sold for the reparation of the church.

Alice Bray, died 1510, from her brass in Chelsfield Church

In 1547 the Chantries Act had provided for the confiscation of all property which had been left for "superstitious" purposes such as funding requiem masses, and to divert the lands to good uses such as the erection of grammar schools, the better provision for the poor, and money for the king's needs. Inevitably this last demand proved to be the dominating one[2].

At Chelsfield, Alice Bray had during her lifetime set up a Feoffment (in effect a trust) which was also summarised in her will[3], to fund an annual dirge and mass of requiem to be celebrated for evermore, for the good of her soul and those of her late husband, her parents and her brother Richard, the former Rector. The rents from the property she had put in trust had covered the annual fees of 12d. to the Rector and 8d. to the Parish Clerk, and the 3s.4d. to be divided at the requiem among the poor of the parish. In fact, this annual event was cut short only 39 years after her death, because in 1549 the "three messuages and one garden and land" (probably at Bucks Cross or Maypole) which were the endowment to finance it were sold to Henry Stapleton at the behest of the King's Commissioners.

Alice had also given to St. Martin's church a small field, the rent from which was to be used to buy new bellropes whenever necessary. This was not considered as a "superstitious" use, and so the rent from the field continued to supply this need until it was sold in 1886 to Henry Thompson of Cross Hall, village shopkeeper and smallholder. The small income from the invested proceeds still goes towards the provision of new bellropes.

The difficult years of transition seem to have passed at Chelsfield without too much turmoil, and so far as I am aware there were no martyrs on either side. Thomas Bacon, who had been appointed Rector in 1532, was a distinguished priest who was a Chaplain to King Henry VIII, a Canon of Ely and a pluralist who was also incumbent of three parishes in Suffolk as well as being Master of Gonville Hall, Cambridge. He successfully tiptoed through the minefield of the changes which occurred during the later years of Henry VIII, conformed to the increasingly Protestant views of Edward VI, survived the reign of Mary I and her strenuous attempts to re-establish the Roman Catholic religion, died neatly in the same year that she did, 1558, and was buried at Chelsfield.

William Gybbins his successor was definitely of the new school, in one way at least, because he was married. By contrast, though, he clung on to the old form of address, being described in the marriage register and elsewhere as "Sir" William, an honorary title often applied to pre-Reformation clergy. His wife Jyllian and only child John were both buried before him, and in his will[4] after leaving bequests to the poor of Chelsfield and Farnborough all residue went to William Perrey and Elizabeth Daites "inhabiting with me". They were evidently children he regarded as his own, and he was very concerned for them, expressing the hope that William might "fall to learning or otherwise in some good art to get his living."

With the death of William Gybbins and the appointment of

his successor there opened a notable chapter in the history of the parish. The Rev. George Smith was presented to the living in 1576, and it was held by him, his son and his grandson, all of the same name, for the next 74 years. The first George Smith was a particularly hard-working parish priest, whose name is encountered at every turn, most frequently as a witness to wills, often made on the testator's deathbed. It was during his time, and I suspect with his encouragement, that Joanna Collet gave her farmhouse called Osborns to the parish, the rents from which were to go firstly towards keeping St. John's chapel and her husband's monument there in good repair.

The popular conception is that after the Reformation people were much less concerned for their parish churches than they had formerly been. This may be the case in some parishes, but at Chelsfield there is much evidence to the contrary, for at least a century after Elizabeth came to the throne. Many bequests of money towards the "reparations" of Chelsfield church occur in sixteenth and seventeenth century wills, while in 1597 John Brasyer the elder, yeoman, left[5] "to the use of the church of Chelsfield for ever 2 sheep to be put in stock", showing that the parish flock was still maintained as it had been in the days before the Reformation. In 1624 Persevale Smale, yeoman, left[6] five shillings "to the buying of necessary books for Chelsfield church."

In mediaeval times it had been customary to encourage the poor to come to the funeral dirge and requiem to pray for the soul of the testator, by leaving bequests of money and invitations to funeral feasts. At the Reformation, the requiem had been discarded as "superstitious," and fees which would formerly have been offered for saying masses were sometimes left instead for the preaching of a sermon. Nevertheless, the wish to have as many people as possible present at a funeral persisted, and there are numerous examples of this in Chelsfield wills. In 1590 Stephen Brasier yeoman left[7] 3s.4d. towards the reparation of the church, and 26s.8d. "to the poor and others assembled at the time of my burial." His widow Margaret, then of Farnborough, in 1594 left bequests[8] to both Chelsfield and Farnborough churches and "to be bestowed at the time of my burial on the poor and for a drinking on my neighbours there assembled forty shillings." She seems to have been a lady of individual character, as she left three "stocks of bees" to various friends. A funeral feast is mentioned in many other wills, and as late as 1649 George Pratt[9] was particularly lavish, instructing his son James not only to distribute 10s. among the poor but also "to bestow in a dinner at my burial 10 stone of beef, 2 of my best wethers, a barrel of beer, and bread proportionable."

This admirable keeping up of a traditional practice came at what was again a difficult period, when the Puritan party had gained the upper hand, the use of the Prayer Book was forbidden, and church buildings suffered injury and neglect. Lists[10] of persons who were suspected of Royalist sympathies were drawn up, and those so identified had to report their movements to the authorities. Chelsfield was reported to have four such "delinquents," among whom appeared Robert Petley, a member of the well-off family to whom I have devoted another chapter.

Robert had a brother, Anthony Petley, the owner of Bucks Cross Farm, who would probably have figured on the list of suspected persons had he not died at about the time it was drawn up – he was buried at Chelsfield on 25 July 1655. His will[11], in which he left the reversion of Bucks Cross to his "delinquent" brother, shows that he was much concerned with the condition of the fabric of the church. Wishing to do "the best of things in the worst of times" he left "forty shillings towards the repair of the Vestry and Chancel of the Parish Church of Chelsfield, the said forty shillings to be employed about laying a piece of timber, mending the gutter or any other work needful to be done between the two roofs of the said Vestry and Chancel and if there be any overplus of the said forty shillings my will is that the same be employed to the reparation of the Vestry aforesaid."

This is interesting as showing the use to which the former chapel on the north side of the chancel was put, after it became redundant for its original purpose at the Reformation. Alas, despite Anthony Petley's legacy, the building must later have become entirely ruinous, because by the early nineteenth century it had been demolished, leaving visible the outline of its steep roof on the east wall of the tower.

A vestry of mean proportions was put up within the site, to be replaced in its turn by the present vestry and organ chamber.

The Smith dynasty in the Rectory of Chelsfield ended with the early death of the third George in 1650, a very trying time for the loyal Anglican clergy. It is remarkable that the unusual monument to the three Smiths, on the south side of the chancel, should have been put up in the following year. Not only does the design emphasise the continuity of the Church of England by copying the tomb of Robert de Brun opposite, but its cryptically worded inscription is avowedly Anglican in tone. Translated from its original convoluted Latin for Arthur Waring by "a distinguished antiquarian," it refers to the three generations as "Three – the same in name, equal in office and most closely united in blood: if I shall say one, I have said all for here lie George Smith the first, the second, the third, and all Priests of the Church of England, Rectors without interruption of this church of Chelsfield...Mary Smith, daughter in law of the first, wife of the second, mother of the third, and Dorcas, wife of the third George Smith, in memory of the dead and in token of affection from a daughter, from a wife, from a mother, erected this monument in June 1651."

During this period the position of the altar (or holy table) became a matter of bitter dispute. The Puritans, influenced by the Calvinists, wished to receive Communion while seated round it, and for that purpose it would be moved to stand lengthwise in the middle of the chancel. This radical break with tradition and the requirements of the Prayer Book was strongly resisted by Archbishop Laud in the years leading up to the Civil War. He ordered altars to be left where they were, and in a new departure decreed that they should be decently railed round to protect them.

The Rev. Robert Milles who followed the third George Smith as Rector in 1650 was not one of the extremists "put in by Parliament" but was presented to the living in the traditional way by the Lords of the Manor, then held by "the heirs of Master Lee." Nonetheless the liturgical arrangements at Chelsfield, in common with those of other parishes, conformed to the Puritan fashion, when the appearance of the interior must have presented an extreme contrast to the scene of only a little over a century before.

After the King came into his own again in 1660, the Anglican liturgy was restored and in 1662 the parochial clergy were required to sign a declaration assenting to the Act of Uniformity and the newly revised Prayer Book. Again, so far as I am aware, there were no martyrs at Chelsfield and although some clergy elsewhere found the new Prayer Book unacceptable, Robert Milles very sensibly conformed, signed the Declaration and remained as Rector until his death in 1692. The Archdeacon carried out Visitations in 1663 and 1670[12] when each parish was given orders to repair the neglect and damage of the Civil War and Commonwealth years, and to restore the proper liturgical arrangements.

Unfortunately the record relating to Chelsfield in 1663 has not survived, but that for 28 July 1670 orders that the Rector and Churchwardens should "provide a patten with a foot to the chalice [and] to cause the Communion table to be railed in as at the Cathedral Church of Rochester, to cause the roof of the body of the Church and aisle to be repaired, to provide a cushion and pulpit cloth for the pulpit, to provide a new Bible, two prayer books, a Table of marriages and a poor man's box. The font to be repaired and a canopy cover to it, the Church to be whited, pavements repaired, the seats throughout the Church to be repaired, the buttresses to be repaired, the steeple to be repaired, bushes and ivy about the Church and churchyard to be cut down and the churchyard to be walled paled or railed." This formidable list, reminiscent of the requirements of a modern Quinquennial Inspection, had to be certified as being completed "at or before the Feast of St. Michael the Archangel next" – giving the Rector and Churchwardens only two months to comply. In addition, they had "to cause the gatehouse entering the parsonage yard to be repaired in the thatching and daubing and the woodhouse to be repaired in the walling."

During the seventeenth century are found the first references to pews being allotted to individual families. Robert Allen, yeoman, asked in his will [13] dated 1643 to be buried in Chelsfield church, "so near my pew as may be." A memorandum entered in the Parish registers in 1675 records that John Bodenham Esq. "did by the consent of the Parish of Chelsfield build him a Seat or Pew in their Parish Church for the better convenience of himself and his Family usually resorting to attend upon the public ordinances of God's worship there and as a gratuity did bestow twenty shillings upon the poor of Chelsfield aforesaid. It is therefore generally agreed upon by the Rector, Churchwardens, and other the Inhabitants of the said Parish that the said John and his posterity in all times hereafter shall have the sole and proper use of the said Pew without placing any others in the same." No doubt this was recorded so formally because the Bodenhams' house, Skeet Hill Farm, was in Orpington, and they evidently attended Chelsfield because it was much closer than their parish church.

When Robert Milles died in 1692 he asked[14] to be buried in the chancel, as many of his predecessors had been, "with as little charge for my funeral as may be, and without any sermon," which was unusual for the times. His successor, the Rev. Michael Petty, was to remain Rector for 59 years, until his death aged 84. He was a bachelor, and his brother John appears to have lived with him at the rambling old Rectory, described in an Inventory[15] of 1712 as "a parsonage house with three barns and two stables with outhouses and garden and orchard." In the same document the entire furnishings of the church are listed as "one silver cup and silver paten, a surplice, a Communion table cloth and napkin, a Pulpit cloth and cushion, a folio Bible and two Prayer Books."

Mr. Petty did not hold any other livings, but he does not give the impression of having done a great deal during his long tenure; his keeping of the parish registers, for example, was distinctly erratic, no baptisms or burials at all being entered in some years and few in others, while the marriage register from 1727 to 1753 is missing. These gaps present serious obstacles to family historians with roots in Chelsfield, but it is interesting to find how many inhabitants in the first half of the eighteenth century travelled to London to be married by one of the parsons detained in the Fleet Prison - until the introduction of Lord Hardwicke's Marriage Act in 1754 they claimed the right to marry all and sundry for modest fees. One such from Chelsfield was Thomas Know, the Parish Clerk, who married Susannah Pegdon of Sundridge in the Fleet in 1747.

The advowson or right of presentation to the Rectory of

Typical 18th century gravestone. Drawing by John Cole c1948

Chelsfield with Farnborough had been a perquisite of the Manor since time immemorial, but Thomas Norton, the Lord who died in 1749, sold the next presentation to Adolphus Meetkirke of Rushden, Herts.[16] and directed in his will[17] that the right of making subsequent presentations should be sold for the highest price obtainable. Adolphus presented his son Charles Meetkirke to the living when Mr. Petty died in 1751 and meanwhile the advowson was bought by All Souls College, Oxford, who have presented all subsequent Rectors, down to the present time.

The living of Chelsfield was a wealthy one, and the Rectors for the next century were well-off Fellows of All Souls, generally younger sons of "county" families in the true English tradition of the period. Dr. Long, for example, Rector from 1781 to his death in 1797, belonged to the Long family of Rood Ashton in Gloucestershire, and evidently spent much of his time at Oxford. A study of the marriage register shows that he conducted only one of the 51 weddings which took place at Chelsfield during his time, leaving this duty for the most part to his curate, the Rev. Robert Jegon. A letter from Dr. Long to John Fuller of Hewitts dated 7 January 1788, photographed by Arthur Waring, is worth quoting in full as it gives the flavour of the times so well:

"Dear Sir

I should have received your account of poor Mrs. Judd's Death one day sooner had your Letter been directed to me at All Souls College instead of my Lodgings, which would have given me an earlier opportunity by a Post of informing you that it is utterly impracticable for me to be at Chelsfield on Friday; I hope however that you will have little trouble in supplying my Place either by Mr. Pratt, Mr. Till or Mr. Brown[18].

I have lately received an Application from the Relations of my late Maid (who still continues in a very bad State of Health)

An impression of St Martin's church interior circa 1790.
Drawing by John Blundell, 2003.

who are unable to assist her, and Parishioners unwilling and as I expect an Application from the Officers for some Relief for her I beg you to direct me what to say; if she should recover she will soon get a Place in this Part of the World, more easily perhaps than if she should be removed to Chelsfield.

If Quaterman has not left my House before you receive this be so kind as to desire him to purchase for me a Razor Strop and dressing at Mr. Mosendie's [?] Oxford Street no. 148. I flatter myself you are all well at Hewetts as you mentioned nothing to the contrary.

I am your affectionate and very Humble Servant J. Long. Oxford Jan. 7th 1788."

It cannot be denied that the eighteenth and early nineteenth century was in general a low point in the history of the Church of England, and a return of 1832[19] made by the then Rector, the Rev. Edward Williams, shows that he also held the two Perpetual Curacies of Uffington and Battlefield in Shropshire - he came of a well-off Shropshire family. He paid the large stipend of £200 per annum to his curate, the Rev. James Williams, who I believe was a relation, and the latter, who had a large family, lived at the Rectory. At that time, service was performed at Chelsfield every Sunday morning or evening, alternately with the Chapel of Farnborough, with a "catechicall Lecture" every Sunday evening through the winter months at Chelsfield. However, "there is also Service at both places on every principal Feast and Festival and at Chelsfield thro' the whole of Passion Week" so that the traditional pattern of worship was maintained, if only at a minimum level of observance.

Box pews, a high pulpit and a western gallery for band and singers were introduced in the eighteenth century. Playing and singing in the old west gallery was a lively tradition in many parishes, and as it was one in which many of the humbler parishioners could join with relish, the passing of this tradition may be seen as a matter for regret. From the chance survival of part of a poster about special services to be held on 1 August 1824 we know that the normal round of services was sometimes augmented. Two sermons were advertised, to be preached "for the benefit of the Sunday

School" by the Rev. James Haldane Stewart of Percy Chapel, London. There were to be special settings of the Te Deum and Jubilate, presumably to be sung by the west gallery singers accompanied by the musicians, and also a hymn by the children.

Fashion in modes of worship and in church furnishing is a fickle matter, and the eighteenth century innovations did not last for very long. They were ruthlessly swept away in the upheavals of the next wave of change, vigorously put in hand by the Victorians.

References

[1] Arch. Cant. volume VIII page 130.

[2] "Kent Obit and Lamp Rents", Kent Archaeological Society Records Branch volume XIV, 1936.

[3] CKS, Rochester Consistory DRb/PWr6.

[4] CKS, Rochester Consistory DRb/PWr15.

[5] PCC, PROB11/90.

[6] PCC, PROB11/149.

[7] CKS, Rochester Consistory DRb/PWr/8.

[8] PCC, PROB11/84.

[9] PCC, PROB11/213

[10] Arch. Cant. vol. XXIII, page 72.

[11] PCC, PROB11/256 – original will, PROB10/832 also consulted.

[12] CKS, Dra/VB6. Kent Records, new series volume I, (Kent Archaeological Society, 1994) has a transcript of the proceedings, and a discussion of liturgical changes by Dr. Nigel Yates.

[13] PCC, PROB 11/220.

[14] CKS, Rochester Consistory DRb/PW39.

[15] CKS, DRb/At15.

[16] All Souls College MSS in the Bodleian Library, Oxford, reference DD C12.

[17] PCC, PROB11/770.

[18] Mr. Pratt and Mr. Till were Incumbents respectively of Orpington and Hayes. Mr. Brown was probably the Curate of Downe of that name.

[19] In the Chelsfield file at the Church of England Record Office, Bermondsey.

Chapter 6

ST. MARTIN'S CHURCH AND THE VICTORIANS

"He bless'd the silver and the gold
Till once more His House is standing
Firm and stately as of old."

- for the Restoration of a Church, from Hymns Ancient and Modern

The Rev. Dr. John Edward Tarleton, appointed as Rector of Chelsfield with the chapelry of Farnborough in 1834 by All Souls College, Oxford, may count as a Victorian because he lived on into the Queen's reign for some 12 years. However, in most respects he was a survival from the eighteenth century; a member of an ancient county family of Bolesworth Castle, Cheshire, he was educated at Eton and Oxford, and became a Fellow of All Souls in 1809 – hence his eventual presentation to Chelsfield.

Dr. Tarleton paid his curates generously to deal with much of the day-to-day work of his living, and passed his time in Chelsfield agreeably enough, in the large old Rectory, now Chelsfield Hospital. This had the distinction of being illustrated in Greenwood's Kent County history published in 1838, described as "a modern house, surrounded by pleasure-grounds and gardens: the interior is remarkably elegant, and contains some very good paintings." I think it was probably Dr. Tarleton who had erected the building, demolishing the historic Rectory which is depicted in a watercolour of about 1797, and in several later drawings in the British Library.

Although from such a wealthy background, Dr. Tarleton appears to have been somewhat unworldly, and towards the end of his ministry his outgoings seem to have outstripped his means, and he was in serious financial difficulties which are referred to sympathetically by Samuel Brooker in his Journal. The Rector died suddenly in 1849, intestate and with outstanding debts, and his affairs were not finally settled for many years[1]. His passing was sincerely mourned in the parish, and the children of Chelsfield village school walked in procession at his funeral.

He took his priestly duties seriously and was a generous benefactor to his parishes, for example presenting church plate to both of them. At Chelsfield he also did a good deal to beautify and preserve the Church, which by his time would seem to have been suffering from some neglect.

In 1836 the chancel was "new roofed," when All Souls College gave £250 towards the expense, and two windows of suitable Gothic design were put in the nave, one on the north and the other on the south at the western end. In the following year, as recorded in the Vestry Minute Book still kept at the church, "the Body of the Church was repaired, and new roofed as far as the first beam – the other part of the roof being thought to be in a state of substantial repair." Dr. Tarleton was the chief subscriber, giving £50 towards the total cost of £259.10s.0d., and he also gave a new west door.

The Vestry Book has a baffling entry in 1838 – "the pews of the Church were painted, and new Chancel gates put up." Betty Coveney, the architect who wrote the NADFAS report[2] from work done by her team in 1987-88, concluded that, however improbably, the expression "chancel gates" referred to the wooden late Gothic style screen which is now across the tower arch. She examined it, and dated it firmly to the first quarter of the nineteenth century. Arthur Waring recorded that old inhabitants remembered this screen having once been in position across the chancel arch, being taken down when that was widened in 1857, and stored for many years in the Rectory barn. Understandably, he thought that it had perhaps been part of the "rodelofte" referred to in mediaeval wills. It was restored to the church in its present place as part of the changes of 1893.

A small volume of 1841 entitled "Instructions and Observations to Churchwardens" is preserved among the records in the Vestry. It contains printed advice by Archdeacon Walker King, and blank pages on which to write observations by successive Archdeacons, recording their visitations and the remarks and recommendations then made.

On 23 May 1844 Walker King recorded that he had "found all things in complete order. It is arranged to put up a new window, of stone, at the eastern end of Collet's [ie St. John's] Chapel."

This was certainly necessary, because in the drawing of 1802 by Petrie[3], it may be seen that the mediaeval east window of St. John's chapel had been partly bricked up, while the upper part of the tracery had been clumsily replaced. The window referred to by Archdeacon King was actually erected in the following year, and it conforms in pattern to those in the south wall of the chancel; again Dr. Tarleton gave liberally towards this improvement, contributing £10 towards the total cost of £45.

The next Rector was the splendidly named Folliott Baugh, another Fellow of All Souls, and with his arrival in 1849 a new chapter in church history was opened. Arthur Waring described the appearance of the interior of the church and the liturgical arrangements as they were at this period, and I cannot do better than quote directly from him: -

"A large part of the floor of the Church was encumbered with the old fashioned high pews... The old fashioned high Pulpit was opposite the south door, between the Memorials to George Morland and Brass Crosby. The floor of the Belfry was not screened from the Church and the Bellringers were in full view of the congregation as they rung from the lower floor in those days. The roof of the nave was ceiled, and continued so until 1896... Some of the old fashioned pews, closely resembled small rooms; seats were fixed all round them and some had a stove in the centre. Some were so high that a child could see nothing of what was going on in the Church. The writer of these Notes [born in 1851] well remembers when quite a little boy, upon the occasion of the christening of a sister, standing on the seat, and getting into trouble for addressing a few kind words to the old family nurse as she walked up the aisle... Both Pews and Gallery were demolished, together with the Pulpit, in 1857; portions of the old pews can still be seen in the Church, as they were used for the lower portions of the present seats.

The writer has found in an old family account book that in the year 1820 there was paid to Mr. Williams, the Rector, £1 towards the Organ, and at the same time 10s.6d. towards a new Barrel for the same. This clearly shows the kind of instrument then in use, which was the usual Organ of the day. This instrument did not require great skill in the playing of it as is evidenced by this entry in the Churchwardens' accounts in 1824 – "Pd. Master Whitehead 1 year playing Organ £1." In 1840 the Vestry resolved that £3 per annum be given to the principal Singers, provided they regularly attended, and instructed twelve of the School children...

In addition to the Barrel Organ, and the Singers, there was at the time a band of instruments which was located in the west gallery. There are several parishioners still living who remember these instrumentalists; the writer well recollects at least one of the performers. An old inhabitant states that William Morgan, who filled various parochial offices, played the Violincello; Stephen Dunmall, of Well Hill, the Clarionet; Bance, Dr. Tarleton's servant, the Violin; and Philip Brooks, at one time parish clerk, the flute. When these instrumentalists were not available, the Schoolchildren sat in the Gallery and led the singing, the Schoolmaster giving the note on a pitch pipe..."

Arrangements like these, common to most parish churches in the eighteenth and early nineteenth centuries, were objectionable to the newer generation of clergy, touched by the teaching of the Oxford, Tractarian or "High Church" Movement. Mr. Baugh, although no extremist, had clearly been influenced in this way, and shortly after his arrival in the parish he instituted a monthly rather than quarterly celebration of Holy Communion. More surprisingly, Samuel Brooker noted on Easter Sunday 1850 that "Chanting of the responses was first introduced this day in Chelsfield Church." This was quite an unusual advance at such an early date; in some parishes the introduction of chanting met with a hostile reception, but that does not seem to have been the case here.

The early Victorian Church was remarkable for a general reawakening to her responsibilities, for the consecration of many new buildings, and for the restoration of even more old ones. Everywhere in England at this period ancient parish churches, many of which had admittedly been neglected during the rather slothful eighteenth century, became threatened in a different way by the well-meaning attentions of clergy, anxious to put them in good order and, even more, to see them conforming to new ideals. High among their priorities was the abolition of the west gallery singers and instrumentalists, and the changes to which this led, sympathetically portrayed in the pages of Thomas Hardy's "Under the greenwood tree," are reflected almost uncannily at Chelsfield.

Mr. Baugh would not have wished to lag behind in adapting his ancient church to new ideas, and in 1856 the Vestry approved a proposal to restore and re-seat the building "in accordance with plans prepared by the architect Mr. Nash." This was Edwin Nash, and it can scarcely be doubted that the reason for his appointment was that he was the first cousin of William Waring of Woodlands, the powerful Lord of the Manors of Chelsfield and Hewitts.

The Nash family, who incidentally were not related to the well-known Regency architect John Nash, came from Farningham, where they have a large and impressive mausoleum in the churchyard. Edwin was a competent architect, and the new church of All Souls, Crockenhill, the Vicarage and the Almshouses there, all of which he designed, are charming buildings. It was unfortunate that when he came to restore ancient churches he was so unsympathetic and ruthless.

A learned journal called "The Ecclesiologist" was the organ of the Ecclesiological Society, which set itself to pronounce judgement on the design of new churches, and whether proposed restorations of existing buildings were considered to be in accordance with its strict principles. In 1857[4] it published a review of the planned restoration of Chelsfield, although it is puzzling that several of the proposals mentioned were not in fact carried out. These include the strengthening of the north wall and the west end by buttresses, and replacing the decayed wooden stairs to the belfry by an open iron staircase.

The most interesting comment is that "in the absence of drawings, we are doubtful whether the existing chancel arch of so ancient a church should be sacrificed as now proposed... We should be glad to hear that this interesting restoration were carried out; but great care is necessary in altering a building of such antiquity."

Accounts of the pre-restoration church are agreed that the old chancel arch was a good deal narrower and lower than that inserted by Nash. This has always been something of a puzzle to me, not least because Nash's plans and the relevant Faculty papers cannot be found. It is only very recently that an explanation has emerged, thanks to a discovery by Susan Pittman of Crockenhill.

Mrs Pittman told me of a volume she had discovered in Canterbury Cathedral Archives. Catalogued as Additional MSS 55, it consists of drawings and plans of Kent churches, mainly in the Diocese of Rochester, with accompanying notes, produced in 1843 by the Rev. Andrew Burnside, curate of Farningham; it includes Chelsfield. I went hotfoot to Canterbury, and on ordering out the volume I was delighted to find that the plan of Chelsfield included measurements, confirming the narrowness of the old chancel arch and giving other useful details of the church as it was before Nash began work. There was also a watercolour of the exterior from the

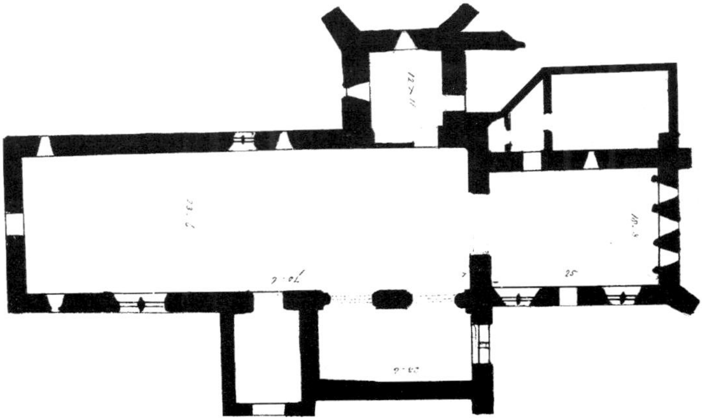

Plan of Chelsfield church by the Rev. Andrew Burnside, 1843

south east, very similar to Petrie's drawing. The really exciting revelation was in Burnside's notes, where he wrote – "This church has a nave opening into the Chancel by a circular arch..." I felt that this could only mean a Norman arch, but since such a feature is mentioned nowhere else, and I do not pretend to an extensive knowledge of mediaeval architecture,

I consulted two experts in this field, John Bailey and Howard Jones, setting out the evidence as I had it.

They both took much trouble over the question, and wrote to me at some length, agreeing in their comments that, on the balance of the information available, in all likelihood the arch destroyed by Nash was indeed Norman, of the same date as the existing walls of the church – that is, between 1080 and 1100. Mr. Jones instanced two cases in Surrey where such ancient chancel arches had met with a similar fate in Victorian times. Whilst deeply regretting the loss of such an historic and unusual feature, it has to be admitted that, from the practical point of view, Nash's arch is much better suited to modern requirements, and indeed it is an attractive feature of the building.

What the parishioners thought of the restored church when they first saw it can now only be guessed at. It seems more than likely that the instrumentalists, ousted from their commanding position in the west gallery, would have been disgruntled at their robust efforts being replaced by the strains of a harmonium, situated in the chancel near the vestry door. Of course, the account of the reopening service in the Maidstone Journal of 19 September 1857 reports that everyone was highly delighted with the changes. The local correspondent commented:

"The old gallery has disappeared, as also the old pews, and instead of the latter, commodious new ones have been erected, extending the whole length of the aisle, affording much more comfort and ample accommodation. The chancel is much improved, and has a very neat appearance; the arch separating it from the body of the church has been heightened; in fact the "time-honour'd" fabric has undergone a complete restoration."

References

1 FRC, Estate Duty records, PRO IR 26/277, referring to a PCC Administration in 1853 and Administration De bono 4 July 1872.

2 A copy of this valuable survey is kept in the Vestry

3 Photograph of original now owned by the Kent Archaeological Society, and at present displayed on their website

4 Volume 18, page 68

Chapter 7

THE GREAT CHELSFIELD INHERITANCE CASE, 1729 - 1733

"James Burton is a pretty fellow ... but I will take care he shall have nothing more of mine but an old pair of shoes which shall not carry him across the parish."

- John Styles's words to his housekeeper on 5 August 1726, a few days before his death.

James Styles of Chelsfield, who owned hundreds of acres in Chelsfield and beyond, died a widower at the age of about 43 in 1710. His ancestors had been solid yeomen, but in his will[1] he styled himself Gentleman. He was much concerned with making provision for his only child John, then aged only eleven, who during his minority was put under the guardianship of James's "good friends and neighbours", Mr. John Petty of Chelsfield and Mr. William Cox of Lullingstone, who were also appointed Executors of the will. They were in one way a curiously ill-assorted choice for those times; John Petty was the brother of the Rev. Michael Petty, Rector of Chelsfield, while William Cox was a redoubtable Baptist. James also requested his "sister Coney" - in fact his sister in law Hannah Coney - " if she please to take upon her the education of my said son and I do desire his said Guardians to pay and allow for his Education what my said sister shall allow in reason."

James very sensibly went on to give directions as to the disposal of his property in the not unlikely event that his son should die under age and without lawful issue. In that case, all his lands were to go to relatives he identified only as "kinsmen" - Hall Farm to Thomas Burton, and his other farms at Green Street Green to John Burton, while the lion's share fell to James Burton. This included not only Lilleys Farm but also "my Manor called Goddington and the Manor House, farm lands and quit rents, royalties and appurtenances thereto belonging" and all residue of lands not otherwise bequeathed, provided James paid some legacies totalling £180 and also took on the payment of an annuity of £10.

In the event, John Styles did attain his majority in 1720, and on 30 November of that year John Petty his surviving Guardian completed the handover of the estate which had been held in trust by making a formal release to him[2] of anything to which he might have a claim "from the beginning of the World unto the day of the date of these presents." I would think that Mr. Petty must have heaved a sigh of relief at having been relieved of his responsibilities. It cannot have been an easy task to have had the oversight of a young man who as soon as he entered into his inheritance began to get through the extensive estate built up so carefully by his ancestors over the past century and more.

As recorded in an abstract of title[3], in 1707 John's father James had laid out £810 to buy Hall Farm at Green Street Green with about 212 acres of land in Chelsfield, Cudham and Farnborough from Captain William Somer. Feckless young John mortgaged it in November 1720 for £600 (present-day equivalent something like £33,000) and moreover did not bother to make any repayments. By the time of his death an additional £150.10s.0d.in interest was due, to say nothing of the principal and interest of £415.3s.6d. on bonds for further loans from various sources.

Although, materially speaking, John Styles must have been an attractive proposition as a prospective husband, he did not marry and, in the event, only lived to enjoy his position as a prominent Chelsfield landowner for a few years. He lived at Lilleys while James Burton his cousin (strictly speaking, his first cousin once removed) lived at Goddington and farmed that and the Chelsfield Hall land.

One of John's neighbours later described[4] him as "of a Negligent and Careless disposition in the management of his Estate and Affairs," a verdict which would certainly seem to be well-merited. Although this led to a great deal of trouble for his relatives, it has fortunately meant that a huge volume of material has come down to us preserved among the records of the Exchequer Court, in which James Burton fought hard over several years to try to prove his claim to the major part of his cousin's estate. The depositions of the numerous witnesses, recorded in their own words, give us an exceptional picture of life in Chelsfield in the 1720s.

The case was brought because John Styles apparently died intestate; his next of kin was the aunt already mentioned, Hannah Coney, but on 15 August 1726 she renounced her right[5] to the administration of his estate. A little later, administration was given to John's cousin James Burton, described in the grant[6] only as a Creditor. An Inventory of the goods, chattels and credits of John Styles was taken[7] going into great detail about the contents of each room, as well as the barns, cart house and yard at Lilleys; the total value arrived at was the very substantial amount of £458.8s.8d., and the Inventory was exhibited in Court in the following February.

Among the items listed in the Kitchen are "three fowling pieces two fishing Rods a sword and whip a Voider and knife Basketts and three fowling baggs." The brewhouse was well equipped, items there including "an Iron Stirrer two Coppers and Irons a Mash tub a pair of Steps three pails etc. hand bowle two seives ...a brass Cock two Earthen Crocks two Earthen Muggs a tray a bill a tap bearer and a Rolling pin." Linen included four nightcaps and "two Child bed Suits."

In the Little Parlour there was a spinnet while the Great Parlour seems to have been very comfortably furnished with "one dozen of Chairs a Large table and hand table a Tea table and the China thereon and two China Punch bowls." The only plants or shrubs listed in the garden were "Gilly flower Layers and old Roots auricula and Missorian Plants - £2.17s.0d."

The document produced by James Burton a year later to account for his disbursements as Administrator [8] discloses one very curious item – "pd. Mrs. Hannah Coney - £100," and someone has drawn in a little hand pointing to this, with the comment "Note – Aunt and had right of Admin: and renounced."

The accounts include items such as the funeral charges (£24.14s.) and 2s. paid to William Alwin "for patting the Grave of Mr. Styles," and with the exception of payments to settle the considerable debts which he had run up, the £100 paid to

Hannah Coney is by far the largest single amount paid out. I find it difficult not to conclude that it was in effect a bribe, to ensure that James Burton would have the predominant position in handling the affairs of his late cousin.

James had already simply taken possession of John's property in Chelsfield and nearby, claiming that the clause in the will of John's father about the disposition of the estate should John die under age amounted to entailment, a somewhat dubious argument. If young John Styles had indeed died intestate, his lands in Kent, subject to the law of Gavelkind, would have to be divided equally among his nearest relatives. In that case the heirs would be the descendants of John's three great aunts, and this had evidently not escaped the notice of a number of such relatives who had filed a suit in Chancery soon after his death.

If James Burton could only prove that John had indeed made a will, and that this was favourable to him, then all his difficulties would be resolved. It was with this in mind that he initiated a case in the Court of Exchequer, and his position is explained at tedious length in the Bill[9] he then submitted, a document of immense size.

The case, as he presents it, is enough to bring tears to the eyes, and James expresses himself very forcibly in describing the way everyone is trying to cheat him of his rightful inheritance. He also pours scorn on the very idea that some of the people who had appeared as claimants to the estate are in fact related to him at all, and goes on about this at length. "...the truth is as they well know that they nor either of them are not nor never were any branch of James Styles the elder's family nor from any of his daughters as now pretended."

As to the supposed will, James states that in August 1726 young John Styles "was Seized with a Seveare fitt of Sickness (but of perfect Sound mind and Memory) whereof he Dyed ...and had only time to make and did make a Short Memorandum or Will in Writing by him duly Executed in the presence of Several Credible Witnesses... Wherein he Declared That it was his Will and Mind (as to the Disposeall of his Estate) That all and every the Devises payments Legacies Clauses and bequeaths in and by his said late father James Styles late Will and Testament... Should for ever Stand and be taken in full force as the last Will and Testament of him the said John Styles."

James alleges that although he knows of the existence of this Memorandum or Will, its whereabouts is being concealed from him by John Petty (the former Guardian), John Tasker (John Styles's lawyer) and William Rolfe, and also by the "pretended" relations William Ebbutt, John Ebbutt, Mary Aynscomb and Susanna Vice, all of whom he names as defendants. He states that they "at a Secrete Meeting among themselves have Severally Sett up some Pretended Right or Title to all the Whole Estate" and pretend that some of them are coheirs to John Styles, whereas the truth was "as they very well know" they are not in any way related to or descended from any of the daughters of James Styles, John Styles's great-grandfather. He is positive that some of them had possessed themselves of the Memorandum and had also carried off deeds and papers of all sorts, and he demands that these all be produced.

After a decent interval depositions were taken on the part of both the complainant and the defendants, and the case grew ever more complex. John Petty and others stoutly denied that they knew of the existence of any will or "memorandum," and indeed Mr. Petty testified that he was sent for immediately on John Styles's death to search for a will. He believed that had there been one it would have been in John's closet at Lilleys, but he could not find one there or anywhere else in the house.

Without going into all the ramifications I will quote here some of the most interesting depositions. These have been put into direct speech to avoid the clumsy circumlocutions of the originals.

Robert Bartholomew of Chelsfield, a shoemaker aged 40 or more, said[10] that John Styles "falling ill of the small pox, I knew that he was indebted to several persons in the neighbourhood in some small sums of money. I went to a neighbour whose name was William Child and desired him to go with me to John Styles' house and endeavour to prevail upon him to make a will. ...but the said Styles sent down answer that he was too ill to see us.

Upon this we went, but 6 or 7 days afterwards and about four days before he died, John Styles sent to me to come to him.

Upon coming into the room where he lay I asked him how he did to which John Styles answered – "Robin John as well as gone only very sore" and then ordered me to open the window and look upon him which I did and asked me how I liked him and afterwards bid me sit down ...and asked me what I wanted with him when he was there last.

To which I answered that we meaning myself and the said Child came to desire him to make a will to know how we should come to our money if it Please God he should do any otherwise than well in this distemper to which the said Styles replied to me and said "Robin I have a will by which I have taken care of every thing, nobody shall loose a penny by me so tell my neighbours."

He further said to me that his cousin James Burton, meaning the Complainant, had been at one Palmers who said that Burton used frequently to enquire what John Styles owed him at which John Styles... said he would alter the property if he lived to get up..."

Other witnesses testified, not very convincingly, that they had heard John Styles say that if he died, then his property should be left to his relations in the way his father had set out in his will. Suddenly, however, the emphasis of James Burton's story changed – miraculously, the Will or Memorandum which all along he had said was in existence had been found, as described in the artless deposition of Elizabeth Staples of Beckenham, spinster, aged 18, taken on 25 May 1730. She was a servant with James Burton and his family, and was not an ideal witness in this case, since it appears from the way she described the document she saw that she could not read, and she had to sign her statement with a cross. Among other matters she deposed:

"When I was in Mr. James Burton's house at Goddington... his daughter Barbara did in my hearing say to her mother that she would tell her news. To which Mrs. Burton answered she did not care how much news if it was but good, to which Barbara Burton replied yes, it was good news, for she had found Mr. Styles's Will...

Upon which Mrs. Burton, seeming overjoyed, asked her daughter where she found it. Barbara answered that it was in the bag of writings her father brought up to Lilleys, which Mr.

Parker [their Attorney] had to look at... Mrs. Burton said further to her daughter after some pause and consideration that she had sometime ago put some money behind or among some books at the house at Lilleys and that she thought she had lost it. She took down the books to look for it, and in putting them up again she picked up a parchment among them which she put into the box of writings. She had since removed the said writings out of the box into the bag above mentioned, and she thought the said Will must have come among the said writings in that way..."

Elizabeth then went on to describe how she had first seen this document on a winter's night at Goddington, two days before it apparently turned up again at Lilleys:

"Richard Parker [James Burton's attorney] and his Man who carries him about, and the said James Burton, all came together to Mr. Burton's house at Goddington. Soon after, they all came into the kitchen there where I was present and then a bag of writings and parchment was emptied upon the table and a candle was called for.

I stood on one side of the table over against the said Richard Parker and while he was looking over the writings on the table I saw the said parchment and writing now produced to me, marked B, as I verily believe... After the said Parker had looked over the said writings they were all put into the bag again and the bag was set by upon a table...

Barbara Burton the daughter found the said John Styles's Will the Monday morning after Parker went to London, in the manner she told her mother. Mr. Burton on that Monday in the evening came from his house at Lilleys to his house at Goddington and there I stood by and heard him read to his wife a parchment writing which was said to be Mr. Styles's Will... I believe this is the same parchment as that now produced and shown to me, it is very like the same as to the size and form and has a little hole in it."

Amazingly, this very document has survived in the Harris Manuscripts, identified in my catalogue as A27. It is written on poor quality parchment and does indeed have a little hole in it; on the outside it is marked B and endorsed with the names of those, including Elizabeth Staples, to whom it was shown "at the time of their several Examinations." Because it passed through so many hands during the time it was an exhibit in the Exchequer Court case the writing is very worn, and illegible in some places. It purports to be a Memorandum by John Styles dated 15 June 1725, reciting the provisions as to property in the will of his father, and confirming that in the event of his own death he wishes these to stand. John Styles signs his name boldly, and the witnesses are Thomas Gunn, Edward Forde and Edward Short of King's Bench Walk.

It will be seen that the date of the Memorandum does not fit in with James Burton's initial story, and the curious circumstances in which it was said to have been hatched are recounted in the deposition of Thomas Gunn who, as testified by others, was the only witness to have survived. On 9 April 1730 he said that he had been a drawer or waiter at the house of one Joseph Pickard at the sign of the Thatched House just inside Temple Bar. On 15 June 1725, at the Thatched House, he was called by Edward Short into the room next to the kitchen where John Styles and Edward Ford were present, in order to be a witness to a parchment.

Evidently doing his best to add credence to an incident which was said to have occurred nearly five years before, he added that Mr. Styles "had on a light Coulered Great Coat, Boots and Spurrs and a Naturall periwig... and as to his Stature was about five foot six or five foot eight inches high... Edward Short was a person of a small Stature with a pale look and had on a suit of Black ...the said Ford was a Tall lusty man but what Coloured Cloaths he had on at the time I cannot now remember."

Thomas Gunn's credibility as a witness was distinctly diminished by the evidence of Barbara Burton, James Burton's daughter, in the same bundle of documents. She deposed that she had known Gunn for about a year past, because he had come down from London to live at Lilleys, where her father employed him as a Bailiff. Thomas had often declared that he wished to go to sea, and James employed him in order to keep him in England "until the matter or difference in this Cause was at an end."

Another telling blow to James Burton's case must surely have come with the deposition of Annes Raworth of Tower Street, London, spinster, aged 38, taken on the part of the defendants on 27 May 1730. She strikes me as a reliable witness, honest and literate, although clearly she was hostile to James Burton and his wife, who, foolishly, had not endeared themselves to her by witholding some of her wages.

She said that she had been John Styles's housekeeper for over five years, and continued there for almost five weeks after his death to look after the house until the goods and other things were appraised. Mr. Styles was taken ill of the small pox on 29 July 1726, and on Sunday 7 August he ordered his Man to go to Mr. John Tasker, his Attorney in Dartford, to bid him come to him on the Monday morning by 6 o'clock to alter his Will, "but Mr. Tasker did not come to Mr. Styles till after his death, not being at home when the messenger went for him..."

On the Monday she asked him if he would have any other person sent for, and the names of Mr. Cozens of Westerham and Mr. Plummer of Sevenoaks were mentioned. In the end Mr. Styles said he would defer the matter and take care of it himself, but soon after this he "was deprived and prejudiced in the use of his reason and understanding by his Distemper" and he died on the following day.

A little earlier he had said to Annes "James Burton is a pretty fellow, he has been to enquire at several houses what I owe but I will take care he shall have nothing of mine but an old pair of shoes which shall not carry him across the parish." She added that he always showed a dislike to Mr. Burton's wife, "and was very uneasy at her coming to his house at any time."

Annes confirmed that Mr. Petty had searched thoroughly for a will, but he could not find one and said it was his opinion that there was none. However, on the next day she herself had carefully searched and looked into "every closet, drawer, box and place in his house and over all his clothes" and found nothing. Not content with this however, she took all the books, parchments and papers in the closet in his bedchamber "and carryed them down on the grass platt in the Court before the door and spread them there to air because the said Complainant Burton had not had the small pox and I am very sure that I did then on the said Grass open every book deed parchment and paper that was in the said closet at that time and I could not then find any will in any of the said places I searched nor amongst the said books deeds and papers taken out of the said closet..."

In even stronger terms she said that she had looked at the outside and beginning of every parchment and she was quite certain that the document then produced, the supposed will, had not been among those she had found. She believed it was impossible that she could have overlooked it if it had been anywhere in the house.

Annes mentioned that about a year before, having some wages due from Mr. Styles and having heard from his gardener that his will was found, she returned to Chelsfield, and saw Mrs. Burton at Lilleys. When the latter asked her if she was not pleased about the will being found, she answered rather pointedly that she was glad, "everyone should have his right..." Mrs. Burton told her the story about how the will was discovered, whereupon Annes flatly contradicted her and "told her I was very positive that it could not be amongst the books because I had opened them all and shaken them on the grass when I took them down to air and Mr. James Burton came to look over them... I told her it was impossible the will could be in the house at Mr. Styles's death."

This must have been a severe shock to Mrs. Burton, who evidently backed off and said that really it did not signify where the will came from and "never would be examined into." However, on the spur of the moment she thought up an alternative but equally unconvincing story as to how the supposed will came to be found, which Annes Raworth recounts without comment.

Meanwhile, John Cotton of Orpington and Samuel Bullock of St. Olave Southwark had been making enquiries in London on behalf of the defendants. On visiting the Thatched House where John Styles was supposed to have signed the Memorandum they found that Joseph Pickard, the landlord at the time of the alleged incident, had also died (there seems to have been a very high mortality rate among those involved in the case) but his widow Jane was still there. She deposed that Thomas Gunn had left his employment at the Thatched House on 15 April 1725, that is, several weeks before he had allegedly witnessed the Memorandum. In support of this she produced a receipt he had signed for all wages due to him up to that date, and she was positive that he had never since been in the building.

The final nail in the coffin of James Burton's case came with a deposition by Joseph Biscoe, a solicitor of the Inner Temple. He stated that on 30 May 1730 James Burton's wife came to see him with a Mr. Harrison, bringing with them the witness Thomas Gunn. Joseph Biscoe asked him outright if he was sure that he had witnessed John Styles's signature when he had been a waiter at the Thatched House on 15 June 1725.

Thomas Gunn confirmed that this was so, and when Mr. Biscoe produced Mrs. Pickard's damning evidence to the contrary "thereupon the said Complainant's wife and the said Mr. Harrison expressed a great concern at what had passed between this Deponent and the said Gunn and went away immediately." I wonder what Mrs. Burton said to Thomas Gunn once they were outside.

In the event, all of Mr. and Mrs. Burton's efforts, and their considerable expenditure on legal fees, were in vain. The purported will was rejected, and the lawyers, who must have gained mightily by the litigation, drew up an enormous "indenture quadripartite"[11] in 1733, confirming the way in which John Styles's estate was to be divided among the heirs in Gavelkind.

This document is a family historian's dream; the estate was divided into nominal thirds, and the proportion of each third to which each of the descendants of the three great aunts of John Styles was entitled are given, together with detailed information about their relationship to each other. James Burton who had initiated the whole affair was in the event entitled only to one third of a third part, plus another one third of a third which had come to him through the death of his brother. He was allocated as his share two thirds of Lilleys Farm and lands in Chelsfield and Lullingstone, and eventually bought out two relatives who had been allocated the remainder.

James does not come over as a very attractive character, and it can only be concluded that he was involved in forgery, but nonetheless I find it difficult not to feel a little sympathy for him. If only the unsatisfactory young John Styles really had taken the trouble to make a will!

James had one son and three daughters who grew to maturity. The son predeceased him and he himself died in 1741, surely a bitterly disappointed man. He was not to know that, by a twist of fate, his grand-daughter Mary would in 1764 marry James Aynscomb of Goddington. James had been left that estate by his mother, one of the successful claimants in the great inheritance case, and through the marriage Lilleys and Goddington came to be reunited in the same ownership.

References

1 PCC, PROB 11/517.
2 Harris MSS A26.
3 Harris MSS J197.
4 PRO, E133/30/33.
5 PCC, PROB 31/42/424.
6 PCC, PROB 6/102
7 PCC, PROB 3/26.
8 Harris MSS A28.
9 PRO, E112/1139/21..
10 This and the remaining depositions quoted are at the PRO, in E133/30/34.
11 Harris MSS A32.

Chapter 8

WILLIAM WARING, VICTORIAN LORD OF THE MANOR

"He was, always had been, and hoped he always would be a preserver of foxes, but it was a trying position to fill, and very annoying to find that their best foxes, when they got to know any extent of country, got killed illegitimately on land where they were not welcome..."

- Mr. Waring in a speech at the annual dinner of the West Kent Hunt in 1868

The Waring family were settled in Wolverhampton in the middle of the sixteenth century, and the ancestors of the Chelsfield line came to Kent via Shropshire and London. Samson Waring of Bridgnorth, who died in 1671, had a son Richard, a lawyer of the Middle Temple, who married Catherine, daughter of the Rev. William Wall, Vicar of Shoreham, and came to live in that parish[1] . The couple had no fewer than 18 children, many of whom lived to maturity; the eighth son, Walter, was of St. Mary Cray, the father of Richard Waring, surgeon, who lived at the house known as Rowlands, at Reynolds Cross.

It was this Richard's eldest son Thomas Waring (1776-1851) who seems to have been born with a silver spoon in his mouth. He was the heir to his grandfather Thomas Fuller's large estate in Farningham, while through his marriage to Sarah, the daughter of John Fuller of Hewitts, he eventually inherited the latter's large Chelsfield estate. John Fuller's Trustees bought the Manor of Hewitts and 80 acres in Chelsfield, Halstead and Shoreham in 1826[2] and Thomas himself added greatly to his estate by his purchase of the Manor of Chelsfield and some 450 acres from Robert Crawford in 1844, thus becoming Lord of that Manor too. Samuel Brooker records how, on 12 January

1845, Thomas Waring "took possession of Mr. Crawford's Pew at Church," marking by this traditional gesture the opening of a new chapter in the parish. On Thomas's death in 1851, the entire property came to his son William, carefully entailed on his issue.

William, born in 1818, was the sole survivor of a large family, all ten of his brothers and sisters having died young and unmarried; family tradition blames this on typhoid from a defective water supply. William, the tough exception to this sorry procession, lived to the age of 86, dying in 1904. He is encountered at every turn when looking at the history of Victorian Chelsfield, and I find him such an interesting character that he well deserves a chapter to himself.

William's appearance throughout his life is well-documented, starting with an attractive coloured drawing of him aged about 14, and continuing with a series of studio portraits at different ages. One taken in the year before his death shows him vigorous and immaculately dressed to the last, with his favourite dog and horse[3]. In the course of a long career as landowner, village squire and keen sportsman he became deeply involved in many local affairs, and we are fortunate that at least a few of his letters have survived, while his views on a number of topics were well aired at meetings of local Hunt and Agricultural Associations, and fully reported in the pages of the Maidstone Journal.

Although I could not resist quoting at the head of this chapter the extract from his speech at the West Kent Hunt dinner, which to me sounds faintly ridiculous, it is rather unfair to do so. He must be judged by the standards and sentiments of his time and class – and he was certainly not a figure of fun but a complex personality, taking his duties as a landowner and employer of labour very seriously.

In a speech to the Orpington and neighbouring parishes Agricultural Association annual dinner, held at the Five Bells, St. Mary Cray in 1866, he stressed the importance of improving the lot of the labourer – "he thought the idea of building cottages was a good one, for he had no hesitation in saying that he had known of cases where labourers had paid the rent of their cottages from the produce of a piece of ground attached to it."

These views are considerably more liberal than those of another Agricultural Association stalwart, Col. Lennard of West Wickham, who said at the 1867 Dinner that although he supported the idea of good housing for labourers "it was a great mistake to build all cottages so as to contain three bedrooms. One result of that practice was that the family themselves lived in one or two of the rooms, and let off the rest; and the consequence was that the landlord really laid out a large sum of money to enable the cottagers to live rent free..." - this at a time when it was not uncommon for farm labourers to have families of nine or ten children. Perhaps this is not surprising coming from Col. Lennard, who at the beginning of the American Civil War had expressed strong admiration for the Confederate cause and had added, "he had himself seen the slaves in America as happy and contented as the peasantry in our own country."

The Bird Scarer by Leslie Collins

At Chelsfield, Mr. Waring's aunt Mary Fuller had been the first to build new cottages for her labourers. In 1824 she demolished what were probably very ancient buildings at Eveshole in the hamlet of Maypole and replaced them with a pair of brick-built cottages, and I think she was also responsible for similar cottages at Back Hill. Some time after the Tithe survey of 1838 she or her successor Thomas Waring (William's father) had the venerable Pax Farm in Church Road pulled down and replaced by a pair of cottages very like those at Maypole and Back Hill.

By a stroke of luck, the original agreement for the lease of one of Pax cottages in 1858 has survived[4] and shows that William Waring let "a Cottage and Garden with the Appurtenances thereto belonging, situate and being at Packs in the Parish of Chelsfield in the County of Kent, lately occupied by George Davis" to Stephen Kimber from

Michaelmas 1858 at a rent of 8s 9d. a month. Stephen died young, in 1884, but although the cottage was a tied one, his widow Harriet and numerous children were not dispossessed. She was still there in 1912, the survey of her cottage[5] showing that she was still paying the rent of five guineas per annum that had been set in 1858. As the landlord (by then William Waring's son Arthur) had to pay rates and taxes and insurance, and was liable for repairs, it is not perhaps surprising that the condition of the building was then described as poor. Harriet lived on until 1923, when she died just short of her hundredth birthday, still at Pax Cottages and no doubt still paying the same rent.

A much more prominent contribution by William Waring to solving the housing problem was the erection in the 1860s of larger, yellow brick pairs of cottages. I believe that all but one of these survive, a tribute to the solid workmanship which Mr. Waring would have demanded for anything built for him. Most of them, which did indeed have only two bedrooms, have been altered and extended to suit modern requirements, some of them very considerably, and the comfort and space thus afforded would astonish their original tenants. Similar in style to the cottages, but on a larger scale, is the farmhouse of Court Lodge Farm, dating I believe from 1863. Different again is the row called Chalkhole Cottages at Maypole, from the same period.

Although naturally conservative in many ways, William Waring had advanced views when it came to anything to do with improving the standard of farming. In a characteristic speech as Chairman at the Agricultural Association Dinner in 1870, which followed the ploughing match held on land in the occupation of Mr. George Phillips at Chelsfield, he gave his views on the subject of ploughing, and then on his favourite topic of improving the lot of the farm labourer :

"His observations in riding over the ground were that it was the best piece of ploughing he had ever witnessed. About eight years ago, when he occupied the same position that he did then, he recollected giving an opinion relative to steam implements. He said he thought he should live to see the steam plough in general and common use, and that in a very few years hence (hear, hear). The great object of agriculturalists was to get the largest possible crop off the smallest space of land, and his opinion was that they could not do it so well with horse as they could with steam power...

There was one question he should like to call their attention to. That was, there appeared to him to be a difference of feeling between the labourer and his employer. He thought the masters should give some attention and consideration to the position of boys when they first left school, to become waggoners' mates. These boys ought to be thoroughly instructed and trained when young relative to the position they were likely to occupy in after years. He thought it was advisable for them to have some place where they could go to after their day's work was ended. In winter especially, they might have a room with a good fire in it, so that they might not be driven to a public-house (hear, hear)..."

Mr. Waring's intensely paternalistic attitude towards the inhabitants of Chelsfield is shown in such expressions of his sentiments. However, despite his forward-thinking views about improvements in agriculture, such as the introduction of steam-ploughs, it is clear that he had no vision of the social order of Victorian times ever changing. In November 1862, the Maidstone Journal reported the ploughing match held on ground at Chelsfield occupied by Mr. William Beardsworth Fox, when:

" notwithstanding it being very cold, there were a great number of persons present, including many ladies of the neighbourhood... There were 42 ploughs in the field, three only of which were iron ones.

After the match, the prizes were announced by W. Waring, Esq. who, in addressing the labourers assembled, said he could congratulate those who had been successful on the excellent work they had done that day. In his opinion some of the ploughing could not be excelled. The money would not be distributed amongst the prizemen that day, but would be sent to them at their homes, and, as soon as time would allow, a framed card also would be sent them, as a memento of the important event, which might be handed down to their children, and their children's children, and would prove, he felt well assured, a stimulus to them to 'go and do likewise.' "

The Agricultural Associations had been founded in the wake

of the serious agrarian disturbances which erupted in Kent around 1830, in an attempt by the farmers and landowners to damp down the fires of discontent, and to ameliorate the lot of the farm labourer. Apart from the money prizes for ploughmen, shepherds and hop dryers, awards were given to men and women for "long servitude" with one master, and to the labourer "who has brought up the largest family without receiving parochial relief," while there were awards too for those who had been married the longest. There was a distinctly patronising tone about the proceedings, including the proviso that money prizes would not be given out on the day because "it had been found that in the fulness of their joy, when surrounded by sympathising friends, the successful competitors were tempted to spend their winnings on their way home..."

By the late sixties, Agricultural Associations were beginning to appear old-fashioned, and in December 1872 a thoughtful article in a magazine of somewhat Radical views called "The Cray" commented discursively that "now the labourers are sufficiently instructed to form unions for their own advancement, associations of this kind are rather out of place, as the agricultural labourer would not, in fairness to himself, and to that free and independent spirit which now enables him to take care of his own interest, and to dictate the terms upon which he will or will not work, like to feel dependent upon the charity and kindness of his neighbours, who hitherto have been willing subscribers to societies having for their object, by means of healthy competition, the relief, in some measure, of his necessities during the cold, dull, months of winter."

This was a somewhat optimistic view of the position of the farm labourer at this period, all unknowingly on the eve of a great agricultural depression, and even the writer admitted that "although we have mentioned the unions as established facts, yet we must bear in mind that they are quite in their infancy..." The topic is a fascinating one on which more research needs to be done, but so far as I am aware no-one was foolhardy enough to try to establish an agricultural Union at Chelsfield at that time. William Waring was the sort of strong character about whom stories abound, and one I recall being told to me by Arthur Eldridge was that even towards the end of the nineteenth century Mr. Waring refused to give his labourers time off to go to an August Bank Holiday cricket match organised by the newcomer Alexander Miller-Hallett on his splendid new cricket pitch at Goddington, on the grounds that Bank Holidays were not meant for farm labourers.

The railway came late to Chelsfield; the line was extended from Chislehurst to Sevenoaks from 1863 onwards,

The Manure Menace by Randolph Caldecott, 1886

encountering great engineering problems, and Chelsfield station was not opened until 1868. The land through which it passed in this parish was almost all part of William Waring's estate, and the station was built in a position which was very convenient for him, whence produce from his farms could easily be taken for despatch to the profitable London market and elsewhere. However, there were increasingly loud grumbles from farmers and fruit-growers in neighbouring parishes that Chelsfield station was very inconveniently situated for them. These rumblings found expression in an indignation meeting held at the National Schoolroom, Knockholt, in March 1868, to protest against "the exclusion of Knockholt, Halstead and parts of adjoining parishes from proper station accommodation."

The speakers urged at great length that a second station should be opened near Wheatsheaf Farm, one of them commenting that "Long Warren [Warren Road] was a very out-of-the way place; it was very difficult of access and was very little known... in that immediate neighbourhood there was not a single house..." Towards the end of the proceedings Mr. Vavassour of Knockholt suggested that a deputation should wait upon Mr. Waring to ask him to improve the road leading to the present station "but the matter was not entertained." In the end, Halstead (now known as Knockholt) station was built as suggested near Wheatsheaf Farm, also on land belonging to Mr. Waring, and was opened in 1876.

To turn to another aspect of Mr. Waring's life, he sat regularly on the Bench as a Justice of the Peace, and on a number of occasions from 1859 to 1862 the reports of these Petty Sessions proceedings at Locks Bottom mention that, among others, C. Darwin Esq. sat with him. This, of course, is Charles Darwin of Downe, a country gentleman as well as a world-renowned scientist and writer – and incidentally a distant cousin of the Kentish Warings.

In the catalogues of manuscript material held at the Centre for Kentish Studies, I was surprised to find a reference to letters from Darwin to a Mr. Waring[6], not further identified. The document in which they appeared proved to be a scrapbook into which letters, mostly from people of local or national prominence, had been pasted; the three from Darwin, which I was delighted to find were indeed addressed to W. Waring Esq., Woodlands, Chelsfield, are preserved in their original envelopes. I was later able to obtain copies of Mr. Waring's responses[7] and the correspondence throws further light on his reputation as an authority on a wide variety of topics.

The query which Darwin initially directed to him in a letter of 6 January 1872 was whether, in studs of first rate greyhounds, all or how many of the puppies were reared. Mr. Waring gave a most detailed reply, writing that "I fear I may not have written very intelligibly – as I am not by any means "great" in that line." Mr. Darwin thanked him profusely, before going on to ask further complex questions which he felt needed to be answered by "some large breeder of greyhounds."

He had to wait some three months for a reply, Mr. Waring

writing apologetically on 13 April 1874 that "I have been much more in Cambridgeshire than Kent... I had a long conversation, on the subject of Greyhounds, with ... one – if not the most successful Public Courser, in the Neighbourhood of Newmarket. He entirely confirms the opinion I gave you. He tells me he never allowed a Bitch to rear more than six Puppies – and not so many, unless she was very healthy and strong... This Gentleman's Dining Table and Side Board are covered with Trophies of all kinds and descriptions, which his Greyhounds have won for him – and he is now in his Eightyfifth year, perfectly hale and hearty, and moves about the country nearly as well as I can myself – and he told me, he did not recollect a single instance of any Greyhound Bitch of his, having a single Male or Female Puppy, when the litter consisted of as many as five or six – and also that it was an equally rare instance, for a Bitch to have less than five Puppies."

Mr. Darwin replied by return, closing the correspondence with the satisfactory comment that "your information accords very nearly with what I have lately received from two other quarters; and it shews me that I had formed an erroneous opinion on the subject."

In 1843 William Waring had married at Wilmington Mary Wall Tasker, the daughter of John Tasker, a brewer of Dartford; the Taskers had long been established in that neighbourhood. William and Mary had five sons, two of whom died young, and six daughters, of whom the eldest, Anne, in a move characteristic of Victorian England, married the Rector of Chelsfield, Folliott Baugh, who was her senior by some 36 years. There is a fine family group of about 1868 showing William and Mary with all the children, on the front steps at Woodlands, a solid, no-nonsense mansion, exactly suited to the Waring family.

There is a wonderful vignette of family life at Woodlands in 1887 in the pages of the diary[8] of Alice, the daughter of Robert Anderson of Cirencester, Lord Bathurst's land agent. She became engaged to Herbert Fuller Waring, William's second surviving son, and on 14 February 1887 noted that "he has gone home today to tell his Father who will probably object to his being engaged. They are swells in Kent and will be angry at his marrying out of his own set ... It is rather an undertaking to get engaged to a man with a tyrannical Father and 5 sisters and 2 brothers who will most likely all hate me."

The following day she noted that "his Father doesn't object though he thinks him most imprudent..." Her fears about the reaction of Herbert's brothers and sisters were also alleviated by receiving "such a nice, friendly, welcoming letter" from his sister Ada. However, the big test came when on 25 February Herbert took her down to stay at Woodlands to meet his father. Alice has a beautiful English style, and her description of the rural scene at Chelsfield is lyrical – " it was a most perfect evening... we went round the front of the house to the "sandy path" – through a little wood which was lovely – the field and trees were getting grey and the Rectory chimneys below and the high pointed roof of the hop kiln were glowing red in the sunset..."

All too soon it was time for the main object of her visit and "we went in to dress for dinner and I began to get very frightened of meeting Mr. Waring who had not yet returned from a visit to Dorking. The gong went before I was ready and that made me worse – but when I got down I found only Ada and Ted [the youngest of the three brothers] in the drawing room. Mr. Waring had come in late, the butler was ill and no wine got up so he and Herbert were doing it. For half an hour we sat there and I got more and more frightened. Herbert came in but didn't dare say very much to me for fear I should collapse. Ada made little remarks which I could hardly listen to and I shook from head to foot and felt very sick.

At last he came in and just shook hands and said "How d'ye do Miss Anderson?" then went to the fire and stood with his back to it and no-one spoke... Dinner was announced, he gave me his arm and in we went, and a ghastly meal it was. He hardly spoke to me for which I was thankful as I could hardly speak and had enough to do to gulp down my dinner. Ted was very good in talking to him a good deal..."

Further details of the household at that time noted by the observant Alice were that they always had "regular schoolroom tea," while she describes Etta (Herbert's sister Henrietta) as "very nice looking and very lively, talks tremendously fast, always bursting with something she has to tell and lisping over

her “ths” and “gs” as they all do.” Perhaps the most remarkable event she notes was on the Sunday of her visit, when:
“...we all went to church. It was a delicious day. Ada had gone to Sunday school; so Herbert, Ted, Mr. W. and I set off alone but met Rose Gordon at the Rectory gate and she came with us. The Warings have a chapel to themselves in church and sit sideways to the rest of the congregation and in full view – and worse than all, come in at a little door in the chancel so we had to walk down the chancel facing the whole congregation and between the choirmen. Ada and I sat in the front seat in the chapel – behind us was an empty seat containing the men’s hats and behind that Mr. W., Herbert and Ted sat! The servants in rows sideways to us!”

I can just remember the pews that Alice mentions, which were removed when St. Martin’s was restored and St. John’s chapel there reinstated in 1950. George Rose’s beautiful plans of the church made in 1941 show how the pews were arranged, while I took a photograph just after they had been removed, showing the marks they had left on the walls of the chapel. What is so very interesting in Alice Anderson’s diary is that the Lord of the Manor, his family and servants evidently entered the church from the priest’s door in the chancel after the congregation and choir had assembled and were respectfully waiting for them. This practice, more typical of the eighteenth century, cannot I think have long survived William Waring’s death, although the pews in the chapel continued to be used by the family.

In this chapter I have done no more than touch on a few of the many aspects of William’s career and character; although, clearly, he was a strong and domineering personality who expected his word to be taken as law in the parish, he was also widely admired as absolutely reliable and trustworthy, his name appearing frequently whether as holding parish offices, an arbitrator in disputes, an Executor or a Trustee. The Victorian gentleman’s concern above all for his good name was shown well when in 1869 he was involved in a legal case over the possession of land at Pratts Bottom[9]. He commented that the piece of ground in dispute was comparatively worthless, but he considered it a matter that affected his character, as it had been hinted that he was trying to rob the defendant.

His funeral in October 1904 was reported at length in the Bromley and District Times: “The oaken casket, upon which had been laid by loving hands, some choice floral tokens of affection and esteem, was then drawn by several of the servants on the estate from the gates into the church ...the children attending the Chelsfield schools, in charge of Mr. and Mrs. W.E. Bailey, carrying their memorial wreath of choice white blossoms and foliage.” The long list of those attending or sending wreaths is a roll-call, not only of the great and the good, but also of humbler villagers: truly they would not see the like of William Waring again.

References

[1] From “A Pedigree of the Kent Warings” by Arthur Waring.

[2] See the chapter on the Petleys and the Manor of Hewitts.

[3] Reproduced in “Bromley and district at the turn of the century,” published by Bromley Borough Local History Society, 2000.

[4] Copied to me by Roy Allchorne of Auckland, New Zealand, a direct descendant of Stephen Kimber, and also of George Davies [spelt Davis in the lease] his predecessor as tenant at Pax Cottages.

[5] Valuation Office Field Book, IR58/14221.

[6] U 1906/Z1.

[7] Cambridge University Library, DAR90:44-45 and 76-78.

[8] The late Mrs. Susannah Bowden, Alice’s grand-daughter, kindly gave me a copy.

[9] Maidstone Journal 30 October 1869

Chapter 9

CHELSFIELD CHARACTERS - A MISCELLANY

"The village has nothing in it worthy particular notice."
- *Edward Hasted, writing of Chelsfield in his History of Kent, 1782*

Hasted and other early local historians devoted little space to those who did not belong to the landowning class, but hidden in Kent's rich archives are many fascinating stories of less exalted people. In this chapter I will try to put a little flesh on the bare bones of some Chelsfield characters.

The Morgan family

The story of the Morgans is one of fluctuating fortunes. The first of this family to move to Chelsfield was Thomas of Eynsford, originally a bricklayer, who became licensee of the Five Bells by 1789. In 1811, as mentioned in the will of John Fuller [1] he was also the tenant of Black Bush wood, The Bells four acres and other land near Skibbs Lane.

When Thomas made his will in 1832 he was living at the house known as Kidders at Bucks Cross; he described himself as "Gentleman" and bequeathed a number of small properties in Chelsfield to his wife for life and then to his children. He also left £1100 standing to his credit in the Bank of England – and in the Bank's records, which are now at the Society of Genealogists he is still described as a bricklayer. However, he had done well for himself and had acquired some existing cottages at Maypole (later rebuilt as the Black Cottages) and had also snapped up some scraps of land nearby on which he built several small dwellings. The tiny site of three of these, which included one called Pepper Box Cottage in the 1901 Census, is the tongue of land at the corner of Jubilee Road and

Aged inhabitants by Randolph Caldecott, 1885

Shoreham Lane, but the buildings themselves became derelict and collapsed or were demolished in the 1930s.

Thomas had six sons and three daughters who survived to maturity, of whom John and James were also publicans, at Bromley Common and St. Paul's Cray. Two other sons, Richard and Thomas, were bricklayers, and the latter moved to Knockholt, where his son and grandsons had their own brickworks near Burlings Lane. The eldest son William became a prosperous farmer, and held office as Churchwarden for some years, besides playing the cello in the church band. By his marriage to Mary, the daughter of John Hills, he acquired the house which his father in law had built on land next to the Five Bells, later known as Brynterion. Mary died childless in 1845 and William married again, and Sarah Ann, the daughter of his old age, was born in 1849.

By her father's will, proved in 1864, Sarah Ann inherited this house and also two cottages at Maypole when she attained 21, with the proviso that she was to enjoy them for life, as should any husband who survived her. After the death of the survivor, if they left no children the property was all to go to William's nephew William, the son of his brother Richard Morgan, and his heirs for ever. Remarkably, these provisions were not resolved until 73 years later.

In 1878 Sarah Ann married Heinrich Sigismund Uhlrich, an artist from Oschatz in Saxony; how they came to meet is a mystery, but he became a well-known figure in the village. Few examples of his work have been identified, but among them he did a sketch and charming finished painting of Lilleys in 1912, evidently as a retirement memento for "Willy" Fox, the farm's tenant. These now belong to Margaret Cobbold, Mr. Fox's great niece, who has kindly supplied me with photographs. A Kentish Times report lists Mr. and Mrs. Uhlrich as having given a painting of Chelsfield to Edward Loxley Waring and Violet Berens as a wedding present in July 1906, and I wonder if this has survived.

Mr. Uhlrich's engraving of St. Martin's church was used on the front of the Parish Magazine for many years, and the only other work of his that I know of is an oil painting of the exterior of St. Martin's church, executed in 1895 and given by him and his wife to their maid, Susannah Foreman, when she married James Scoble. It had descended to her niece Edna Wilderspin, who lent it to me to copy shortly before she died in 1997. I was touched to find that in the 1901 Census Susannah's young daughter Gladys was staying with Mr. and Mrs. Uhlrich, and they seem to have been an amiable and well-liked couple. The late Oswald Bowen told me that his father, Percival Bowen of Wheatsheaf Farm, commissioned a portrait from Mr. Uhlrich, but that the painting was never forthcoming.

His artistic temperament does seem to have made him rather vague, and even by 1914 when Brynterion was surveyed[2] it was described as being in very bad repair, inside and outside. I am told too that Mr. Uhlrich suffered some persecution in the village during the Great War because of his German origins. He continued to live at Brynterion after his wife died in 1927, and there is a letter of 1935[3] throwing a sad light on his declining years – addressed by United Dairies of Orpington to Mrs. Norman Butler of Chelsfield House, it thanks

Plan of Cross House, by James Gudsell, 1811 (David & Mary Lambert)

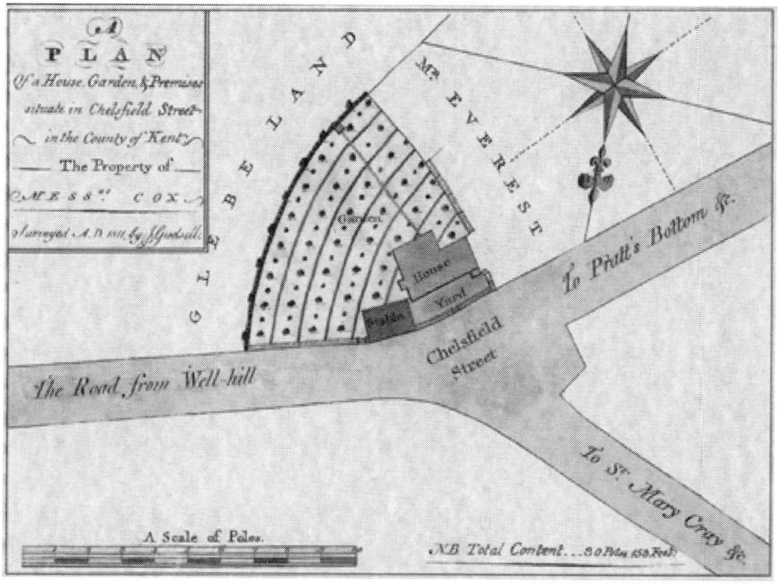

her for alerting them to the number of empty milk bottles at Brynterion, confirming that 1,606 had been collected. Poor Mr. Uhlrich had a tragic end - in 1937 when he lay in hospital in his last illness his house was burnt down, perhaps deliberately[4].

William Morgan's nephew and heir, a fruit-grower, had had five children, who were his heirs on his death in 1923. By the time Mr. Uhlrich died the Maypole cottages seem somehow to have passed into other hands, and his Morgan inheritance I believe consisted only of the derelict site of Brynterion, on which a new house was built after the Second World War.

Oddly enough, there was another lengthy inheritance saga involving the Morgan family in the village. William Hills, the son of that John Hills who had built Brynterion, was a bachelor, and among other properties he owned Cross House in the village, where he and his spinster sister Sarah ran the Post Office. She died in 1863 and he in 1868, leaving a remarkable will on which I have commented in the chapter about Worlds End. He left Cross House on trust so that his domestic servant Mary Morgan might enjoy it rent-free for life.

On her death it was to pass to any children she might have, and failing that, to her brother Thomas Morgan and his heirs for ever. William also left her all the household goods in Cross House and £2000 "in recognition of the faithful service which Mary Morgan has rendered to myself and to my late sister Sarah Hills."

This Mary was a first cousin of Sarah Uhlrich, and the handsome legacy from her employer enabled her to live comfortably at Cross House for the rest of her life. She never married, and the Census returns show that her family shared to the full in her good fortune. In 1881, for example, her mother, her sister Sarah, her brothers James, John and Henry (all described as farm labourers) a nephew and a niece were all living at Cross House with her.

Thomas Morgan, Mary's brother and heir who rented Osborns from the church, also farmed other land and was an official of the Probate and Divorce Court. In the event, Mary outlived him, not dying until 1921, when she was aged 89, and in accordance with William Hills' will, Cross House went to the only surviving child of Thomas Morgan of Osborns, Sarah Ann, the wife of Charles William Reedman, a Scottish Master Mariner[5].

Mr. and Mrs. Reedman, who were then living in Glasgow, put the premises up for auction in September 1921, described as comprising two tenements, one being "a capital shop... in the occupation of Mr. W. Stacey, Postmaster, where the business of THE VILLAGE POST OFFICE and General Store is carried on." The remaining portion was the part in which Mary Morgan had lived, and the whole was sold for £700, to Herbert Smith.

Faithful servants

In Dorothy Cox's "Book of Orpington" is a photograph of long-serving servants of the Waring family of Chelsfield, which she dates to about 1880. However, documentation belonging to Beth Nichols, the grand-daughter of Arthur Waring who inherited the family home Woodlands in 1904, shows that in fact the group was taken outside the house on 6 April 1908. The names and length of service of each servant are recorded, showing that some of them had come out of retirement for the occasion, among whom Tom Blundell had worked for the family from 1847 to 1905, while Jack Dunmall was apparently still working after 65 years service.

Mrs. Nichols when little often stayed at Woodlands, she and her brother travelling on the train from Maidstone with their Nanny to Swanley Junction, where they would be met by the Woodlands carriage. She has vivid recollections of the final years of the old regime, when the house was still kept up in the traditional way, and the female under-servants walked in a sedate procession to church on Sunday mornings, wearing bonnets provided by her grandmother Agnes Waring.

Mrs. Nichols seldom saw her grandparents, and never ate a meal with them. In the evenings Georgiana Ferrier, the head housemaid, came up to the Nursery so that Nanny could go and get her supper. Georgiana had come down from Nairn to Kent at the age of 16, and she sang her charge to sleep with Gaelic lullabies. A highlight of every visit was a tea party in the Servants' Hall; when the youthful Beth Waring, "spoilt rotten" by the servants as she says, thought she was too grown-up to wear a bib, Albert Hill the butler shamed her into it by putting on a large napkin himself.

The late Susannah Bowden, Mrs. Nichols' cousin, lent me two family albums, one of which has photographs of Chelsfield taken in 1900, including individual pictures of servants and retainers who are not in the group photograph. Among these are Underwood the coachman, and Mrs. Slater and Mrs. Martin, who lived at Bucks Cross, noted as having scrubbed the floors at Woodlands on Saturday mornings.

Before the Great War altered the social scene the Warings, like all upper class families, expected deference as well as hard work from their servants. Service in the big houses of the period must have been rather claustrophobic, although with a strong sense of belonging to a community. In the uncertain conditions which existed before the birth of the welfare state it was prized as a steady job for life and if the employers were conscientious – as I believe from the evidence that the Waring family were – the benefits far outweighed the drawbacks.

The plight of the poor.

It has never been a simple matter to deal with the problem of the poor, the sick and the weak-minded. The harsh rules of the Elizabethan Poor Law obliged parishes to maintain their own paupers. A whole range of documents exists relating to the way parish Overseers and local Justices tried to establish the legal place of settlement, while parish chests often contain supporting documentation. In Bromley Local History Library are several bound volumes of the surviving Bromley Petty Sessions papers for the district[6], recording the examinations of people who were paupers, or thought likely to become paupers, and many sad tales are to be found in their pages.

One aspect which comes over strongly, is the uncertainty of livelihood of large numbers of people, and their reliance on the goodwill of their employers. When James Cope of Cudham was examined in 1827 he said - "my father George Cope is now residing and legally settled in Chelsfield, and I was born in that parish. Over 20 years ago I, when a lad, lived with Mr. John Gravett of Chelsfield, farmer, for about 6 years, without agreement for wages. My master found me in clothes and victuals and some pocket money and I slept at Mr. Gravett's, and I have not since done any act to gain a settlement..."

The most prosperous of the Chelsfield inns was the Bull's Head at Pratts Bottom, once a busy coaching establishment. Employment there was on a distinctly casual basis, as recorded in the words of Thomas Hines of Bromley in 1831 – "About 14 years ago, being single, I asked Mr. Tibbs of Pratts Bottom if he wanted a waiter – he gave me only victuals and lodging and I was to have what I got by gentlemen. I served him 2 years, slept at his house and received what gentlemen pleased to give me..."

Then as now, those who were more spirited and literate were better able to stand up for themselves. One such was Mary Rudland of Southwark, whose letter to the Overseers of the Poor of Chelsfield dated 31 August 1835[7], threatening to send her son back for them to maintain, is a masterpiece of gentle blackmail.

She wrote that "my son Robert Rudland is now of an age that he might earn a trifle towards supporting himself and I could get him plenty of situations here but I am unable to purchase him any clothes, as we have a large family and his Father in law [stepfather] was all Spring out of work. Had you not stopp'd his allowance, that you were in the habit of sending, I should ere this have cloathed him well enough. I trust you will take this into consideration and send me a trifle otherwise I shall be obliged to send him down that you may maintain him and get him Employment..." Unfortunately the Overseers' accounts for the period have disappeared, so it is unknown if Mrs. Rudland's efforts were crowned with the success her literary skills deserved.

An Edwardian tragedy

William Elias Bailey came to Chelsfield in November 1883 as Master of the village school, in which his wife Lucy also taught, and later their daughter Annie. Mr. Bailey was an important figure in village society, being elected to the first Parish Council in 1894, on which he acted as Clerk. He was also choirmaster of St. Martin's church and incidentally did a thorough, neat job as Enumerator for the 1901 Census when, rather endearingly, he started with his own household in the Master's house next to the School. The school prospered under him, and he kept the logbook[8] meticulously, noting all the little incidents which add much to our picture of village life at the period.

On 12 July 1906 Mr. Bailey joined a party of 34 substantial inhabitants of the district who were members and friends of the Orpington, St. Mary Cray and District Fire Brigade, on their annual outing to Brighton. They had hired a double decker omnibus with an open top for the occasion, and they passed through the countryside in fine style at 10 to 15 miles an hour until they started to go down Handcross Hill in Sussex. There the brakes failed as they gathered speed, and when the driver went into reverse gear there was a huge bang, and part of the underside fell away.

Those on the top deck tried to get down the stair, and two threw themselves off, just before the vehicle lurched out of control and rushed straight into a large oak tree. The upper deck passengers were catapulted in every direction, six of them being killed instantly and three dying shortly afterwards.

Mr. Bailey's fate was particularly unpleasant, as he was so badly injured that it was considered inadvisable to move him to hospital, and he remained at the Red Lion, the village inn close to the site of the disaster. The District Times reported that "for over two days a strenuous fight for his life had been made by Dr. Sidney Matthews and two nurses, and for a little while there was some hope " but his case was hopeless. Astonishingly, the Inquest on the nine dead was held at the Red Lion, when the Coroner had to ask the Jury to be as quiet as possible as Mr. Bailey was in the next room. He died there in the afternoon while the proceedings were still in progress, the Inquest on him being commenced in the evening.

The accident shocked the whole area, and the District Times carried harrowing details. "With the funeral of Mr. William Elias Bailey, of Chelsfield, the grave closed over the last victim of the Handcross disaster" read the report of his funeral, when the local Masons, of which body he had been a prominent member, turned out in force, and the Rector, the Rev. J.J. Baddeley, was assisted by his predecessor, the Rev. H.B. Barnes. On the Sunday Mr. Baddeley spoke about Mr. Bailey at length, commenting as a final accolade "his last Government report showed that their school had earned the "Excellent" merit grant."

As the last note written in the logbook by Mr. Bailey records, the village school "Broke up for 4 weeks "Fruit picking" Holidays" on 6 July. In the next entry, on 7 August, Mr. R.E. Waite wrote, "Took temporary charge of this school owing to the sad death of Mr. Bailey..." School life went on much as before, Mr. Waite noting that on that day there was a very poor attendance, only 112 from a roll of 148, so perhaps the fruit picking, an activity vital to the cottage economy at Chelsfield, had not yet been completed.

References

1 PCC, PROB11/1624.

2 PRO, IR58/14220/70.

3 In St. Martin's parish chest, copied for me by Philip Lane.

4 See Derek Sheffield's "Till the end of time" for a photograph of Brynterion and more about Mr. Uhlrich.

5 In the Cross House title deeds, lent to me by David and Mary Lambert.

6 See the index by Elizabeth Silverthorne, NW Kent Family History Society publication.

7 Now with Chelsfield Parish chest documents at Bromley Local Studies Library.

8 Peter Heinecke gave me copies of this fascinating document, 1883-1906.

Chapter 10

MORMON EMIGRANTS FROM CHELSFIELD

For some must push and some must pull
As we go marching up the hill,
So merrily on the way we go
Until we reach the Valley-o!
- *Mormon emigrants' song*

Before we moved from Orpington to Tunbridge Wells in 1960 my knowledge of the Mormons had been practically nil. At that time, however, my wife noticed an advertisement in our local paper, inserted by a lady in Utah asking if anyone had any knowledge of the Jackson family of Chelsfield.

I was naturally intrigued by any reference to "my" parish, so I wrote to the advertiser, Mrs Trenna Butterfield of American Fork, thus beginning a long correspondence with her. This soon led to her putting our names on the books of the Genealogical Society of Salt Lake City as researchers.

Over the next 30 years my wife and I did a vast amount of genealogical work for the Society, and also for private "patrons" as the Americans rather grandly refer to clients. This, of course, covered the whole of Kent, and sometimes extended elsewhere, but whenever the searches veered towards Chelsfield the "patrons" were assured of special attention.

I was fascinated by the entirely new slant given to my picture of life in Victorian Chelsfield, by my contact with the American Mormons.

The Mormon movement had its origins in a vision vouchsafed to Joseph Smith in America in 1820, which revealed to him that Jesus, after his Ascension, had appeared on the American continent to descendants of families who had arrived there from Jerusalem some 600 years B.C. As early as

1837 the first party of Mormon missionaries visited England, and began to make converts. The fact that the Mormon message was centred on a specific American revelation led directly to many English converts wishing to emigrate there. The Mormons' belief in the virtues of the family, and of the duty to offer dead ancestors the opportunity to convert to their faith, led directly to their interest in genealogy.

It was perhaps ironic that an old-fashioned High Anglican such as myself should have become involved with a religious body having few points of contact in matters of belief and practice. In fact, though, it seemed to work very well.

At least in Kent, many of the early converts were nonconformists, generally living in the outlying parts of parishes where, before the revival in the Church of England which began in the 1830s, the poorer inhabitants had to some extent been neglected by their parish priests. This is certainly exemplified in Chelsfield parish, where the Jacksons, Sineys and Staples all lived in the hamlet of Pratts Bottom, which had no effective Anglican presence until 1886.

A Meeting House Certificate[1] for a nonconformist place of worship in Pratts Bottom was granted in 1810, and the first Methodist meeting in Chelsfield is recorded on a pane of glass formerly at Hewitts Farm as having taken place there in 1812. In the course of the nineteenth century Methodism became a force in the parish, with a strong following among the farm labourers. The Reverend Folliott Baugh, the Rector, wrote with disarming frankness to the Archbishop in 1876[2] that "the agricultural labourer will prefer any kind of dissenting place of worship to that of the established Church which he associates with the idea of authority and oppression." Nevertheless, there were those who felt that the Methodists had lost some of their Apostolic fervour, and to them the Mormons made a particular appeal.

The brief "Biography of the Thomas Jackson family" which Mrs Butterfield sent me, states that "Great grandfather [Thomas Jackson of Pratts Bottom] was a builder and contractor by trade, and a Methodist by faith until he was converted to the Latter Day Saints' church, through some Elders who were missionaries to that land. One of them administered to their daughter Sarah for her deafness, and she was healed. All of his family joined the church, including many relatives."

The other feature common to many of the early converts is that they were often from families which had come down in the world, whether through their own shortcomings (like the Udalls of Goudhurst, in the Weald, who had "drunk away the farm" and whose old mother had died "crazy in a van") or - more frequently - through social causes which were beyond their control. This latter was the case with the Chelsfield Jacksons.

This family had been prominent inhabitants of the lower part of Chelsfield parish from at least the 17th century. Jacksons were at various times the well-to-do tenant farmers of Cacketts, Washneys and Fairtrough, whilst relations farmed extensively in Cudham. When Richard Jackson of Fairtrough wrote his will[3] in 1792 he described himself as a yeoman, and this was well merited, since his monetary bequests alone totalled £700. The lease of the farm, with cattle, crops, husbandry gear and all residue was left to his widow to enable her to maintain herself and to educate and bring up the younger children.

Clearly, at that stage the Jacksons were in comfortable circumstances, but things soon began to go wrong for them; I believe that, ironically, one of the underlying reasons for this was the general decline in the incidence of child mortality. Until the later part of the 18th. century it was commonplace for only one or two children in a family to survive to adulthood, perhaps out of ten or twelve. When, because of better (if still rudimentary) conditions more began to live to maturity, the new situation affected all sections of society. The upper classes - the Hart Dykes of Lullingstone Castle are a local example - could postpone the consequences of having to make provision for a dozen offspring, by mortgages, advantageous marriages, or breaking the entail and selling outlying portions of the estate. Except, perhaps, for the very occasional judicious marriage, no such options were open to less fortunate families, who soon made the all too easy transition from comparative affluence to grinding poverty.

The sad story of George Jackson is an example of this progression. He was born in 1767, the eldest child of Richard

Jackson of Fairtrough mentioned above, who left him £150 in his will. His mother continued to farm Fairtrough for some years, but so far as may be seen George did not follow her there. He married, and from 1794 onwards had ten children, most of whom survived and must have been the main factor in impoverishing him and his wife.

The Jacksons were more fortunate than most families, since they had acquired two small freehold cottages at Pratts Bottom, which they contrived to hang on to until well into Victorian times. However, the 1841 Census returns for Pratts Bottom show our poor George Jackson, a widower whose occupation is given as farm labourer, living in one of these properties with his son Thomas (the emigrant) and the latter's family. There were seven people in all in the tiny dwelling, and two more grandchildren arrived later in the forties, to add still further to the overcrowded conditions.

Thomas Jackson's wife was called Rejoice Staples, and her family also lived in Pratts Bottom in the 19th century. Although we have not been able to trace them back with certainty before the mid-18th century, I am sure beyond reasonable doubt that they are descended from the Staples or Stables who were wealthy landowners in Orpington and Chelsfield from at least the late Middle Ages. Some of them too managed to retain small freehold cottages which gave them a little more independence than the average landless farm labourer of the 19th. century.

We are fortunate in having another, more detailed, account of the Jacksons in a typescript given to me in 1971 by Sharlee Doxey, a descendant of James Jackson of Pratts Bottom. We went with her to Fairtrough, and were very kindly invited in to see the house where her ancestors had lived 200 and more years before: she could hardly speak for emotion.

The account, written by James' son Harvey Jackson, states that "from 1862 to 1872 father planned to return to England to baptise and be the means to assist those of his kindred to emigrate to America. By 1872, he had acquired stock and land, built a home and had three wives and quite a number of small children... it seems those pioneer fathers didn't hesitate to place increasingly difficult loads on their wives when they went off on foreign missions... father's appearance when he went on his return mission to England was rather noticeable. He wore home-spun, home-made clothes. The story tells that his trousers were over-large, baggy at the seat and, of course, unpressed. When he went aboard and registered and paid for first-class passage, no doubt there was surprise and eyebrow-lifting among the first-class passengers. But he felt he was equal to anyone as he had six hundred dollars in his pockets, which was quite a sum in those days. He was never seasick... James Jackson baptised 8 of his immediate family and at that time about 75 of his kindred joined the church. He returned to Dixie and about 3 or 4 years later many of his relatives came to America..."

The contrast between existence in an overcrowded cottage in Chelsfield and the free life awaiting the emigrants in America hardly needs to be emphasised. However, many of the families had adventurous journeys, and for some of the Jacksons these included attacks by Indians and having to make wide detours to avoid the areas fought over in the Civil War. Nonetheless for the majority - at least those from Chelsfield about whom there is documentation - it was all worthwhile, and one emigrant who revisited the land of his ancestors in 1875 made the telling comment that "the laboring class of people in England are afraid to stand and talk to anybody 5 minutes at a time..."

Apart from the inter-related Jacksons and Staples there was another large family group of Mormon emigrants from Chelsfield, the Hollands. I came to know of them also via our genealogical work, through Jerry Haslam who is descended from them, and also from many other Chelsfield families as one gets further back. Jerry (Dr. Gerald Haslam, now lecturer in history at Brigham Young University) visited England in 1973 with his brother Craig, and we had a wonderful time visiting various ancestral spots, including the White Hart at Bopeep and the disused churchyard at Halstead.

True to the general pattern, many of Jerry's ancestors had been well-off yeomen in past centuries, not least the Allens of Hewitts and the numerous Brooks clan. Like the Jacksons and the Staples, the Brooks had declined in status, but had hung on to small freehold properties, until these too had had to be sold for the proceeds to be divided among numerous heirs. The immediate ancestors, the Hollands family, who were comparative newcomers to Chelsfield, were at the dreary level of farm labourers in Victorian times, with little hope of ever getting out of the rut; at the time of the 1871 Census their small cottage at Bopeep housed the parents and 6 children.

It was Jerry who first made me aware of the material which is deposited at the Salt Lake City Genealogical Library, which records the meetings of Mormon Councils in England. His notes taken from these, about his own ancestors, showed the existence of a very active Mormon group in Chelsfield from the mid-fifties onwards.

It was a surprise to me to find references to a Joseph Siney as being a person of some consequence in that community, because although the Sineys were familiar to me, it had been in quite a different context. They would seem to have been rather a shiftless family, sometimes in trouble at the Petty Sessions, frequently the recipients of parish relief, and some of them indeed living at one time in the old parish poorhouses at Pratts Bottom. In 1853 these ancient buildings were described as being "in a most dilapidated state, and quite unfit to be inhabited by Human Beings.[4]" The Sineys showed much originality in the Christian names they gave their children - Lorenzo and Angelina, for example. I have the impression that they were the sort of family about whom the Guardians of the Poor (roughly the Victorian equivalent of Social Workers) would cry - "Oh no - not the Sineys again!" Clearly, however, given a chance, one of them at least rose to the occasion when given responsibility in the organisation of his newly adopted religion, as shown in the minutes of the meetings of the Bromley Branch Council, held at Pratts Bottom[5].

On 3 June 1858 "Brother J Siney reported the saints [that is, the Mormons] in Chelsfield to be most in a weak state particularly in regard to tithing wherewith they did not all comply..." In 1859 Jane Hills (an ancestor of Jerry Haslam) was summoned to attend the Council meeting "to answer the Charge that was against her as regard hard feelings against Bro J Siney she said she would make reconciliation with him if he would show the walk of a saint..." It is clear that Joseph Siney and other members of the Mormon community in Chelsfield took their new responsibilities very seriously, and did not flinch from visiting backsliders to rebuke them for their unsatisfactory behaviour, whether in the sins of the flesh or in failure to conform to the precepts of their new religion in such matters as almsgiving or marriage.

It is strange that there seem to be few references to the Mormons in the local press of the time - in fact, the only one I have yet found in a fairly wide search in mid-Victorian times is in the South Eastern Gazette of 18 August 1857. This reports under the heading "Baptist anniversary at Farnborough" that Mr Webb of Farnborough "has engaged to examine the Mormon doctrine "God is a natural being", or, in other words, the book which the Mormons circulate, entitled "The Absurdities of Immaterialism" by Orson Pratt, at Pratts Bottom, Chelsfield, on Sunday afternoon next, at 3 o'clock, in the open air, if the weather is propitious, and will preach again in the open air, on Well-Hill, at 6 o'clock." Unfortunately I have not found any reference to what actually happened on this occasion.

It is tantalising too that I have not so far unearthed any evidence about the way in which the new converts fitted into the close-knit village community. They must have found it difficult to keep to the strict letter of the Mormon law, and in fact many parents who professed the new religion also conformed to the Church of England, at least to the extent of having their children christened at the parish church.

Among these were John Cooper Hollands and his wife Sarah Ann née Hills, nine of whose children appear in St. Martin's baptismal register between 1861 and 1874. Family papers record that eight who survived to maturity, and their mother, emigrated to Utah. A detailed biography of the most successful of the children, Thomas Hollands - later a Bishop in the Church of the Latter Day Saints - was published in 1902, and it records that both of his parents "became members of the Mormon church in 1850, and were among the first to join in England. The father died on March 2 1874, leaving the mother with 11 children on her hands... In 1876 [Thomas] came to Utah with a company of Mormon emigrants... he saved his small earnings, and in the fall of 1882 he had saved enough to bring his mother and five more of the children to Utah... He also borrowed 110 dollars and brought a sister to Utah from Pennsylvania. One sister remained in England, where she was married... Being the head of the family, he rented a large farm near Nephi, on which he gave his younger brothers employment, and there established the family..."

The early Mormons did have a very independent spirit, and I came across a manifestation of this when going through the files of the Maidstone Journal. On 26 June 1869 this carried a report referring to Jane Hollands of Chelsfield, aged 13 (the eldest child of John Cooper Hollands and Sarah) who was up before the Magistrates charged with "writing indecent words on the palings around the residence of W. Waring Esq." Mr Waring said in Court that "for a long time they could not discover by whom it was done. At last the child now before them was detected in the act of so doing. It was a shocking thing to see a child guilty of so shameful a thing, who had been properly educated in the village school." The Magistrates called in the parents, and cautioned them that "it was their strict duty to check and punish such wicked conduct, and as a caution a fine of 5s. would be inflicted."

Writing rude words in public places is not very nice conduct, but in this instance I must say that my first feeling was one of astonishment, even reluctant admiration, that anyone should have dared to do this on the property of such a redoubtable figure as William Waring of Woodlands. I wonder what he had done to upset Jane, and what were the "indecent" words?

The incident must have been deeply embarrassing to her parents, not least because Mr. Waring was their landlord. However, it does not seem to have done any lasting harm to Jane, who married in 1875 and later joined the family in Utah. Her photograph certainly portrays someone who would come out of her corner fighting, and both her great great nephew in Utah and William Waring's great-granddaughter in England found the episode entertaining when I told them about it.

References

[1] CKS, Dra/Am 1/87, 88, 95.

[2] LPL, Visitation returns VG3/5a.

[3] PCC, PROB 11/1225.

[4] In a letter to the Poor Law Commissioners, quoted by Arthur Waring.

[5] Extracts from the minutes, as well as the information about the Hollands family, have been communicated to me by Dr. Gerald Haslam.

PLATE 1 *Gertrude Dunmall at Hollybush Lane, a watercolour by Miss Waring c.1893. These cottages were demolished and the Black Cottages built on the site in 1898. [Sidney Dunmall]*

PLATE 2 *Edwin, Elizabeth and Lesley Foreman at Rose Cottage, a typical Lullingstone Estate dwelling at Well Hill, c1912 [Mrs.Marjory Smith]*

PLATE 3 *An ancient "yeoman's house" at Green Street Green. Later divided into tenements, it was demolished in about 1914. [Bill Morton, also Philip Lane Collection]*

PLATE 4 *Worlds End Farm being demolished in 1962 [Derek Stoyel]*

PLATE 5
William Hills, postmaster, owner of Worlds End and Cross House, died 1868 [Arthur Waring]

PLATE 6 *The monument to Robert de Brun, Rector of Chelsfield, died 1417.*

PLATE 7 *Arthur Thomas Waring, 1851-1920: Lord of the Manors of Chelsfield and Hewitts, J.P, Alderman, and historian of Chelsfield. This photograph of c1877 shows him in his Kent Volunteer Artillery uniform [Mrs. Susannah Bowden]*

PLATE 8 *The monument at Chelsfield to Peter Collet, died 1607, his wife Joanna and family.*

PLATE 9 *Chelsfield Rectory, a watercolour of c1797. Demolished c1830 when a new Rectory (now Chelsfield Hospital) was built on the site (author's collection).*

PLATE 10 *William Waring aged about 14, a watercolour of 1832 [Mrs. Beth Nichols]*

PLATE 11 *William and Mary Waring with their children, taken on the steps at Woodlands c1868 [Mrs. Beth Nichols]*

PLATE 12 *Mrs. Louisa Slater, laundress, who lived at Laundry Cottage, now 3 Bucks Cross Cottages, 1900. [Mrs. Susanna Bowden]*

PLATE 13 *Georgina Ferrier, head housemaid at Woodlands, 1900. [Mrs. Susannah Bowden]*

***PLATE 14** James Jackson, a Mormon emigrant, born in Chelsfield in 1826 [Sharlee Doxey]*

***PLATE 15** Fairtrough Farm c.1895 [Mrs.Margaret Cobbold]*

PLATE 16 *Elizabeth, wife of Robert Crawford of the Court Lodge, 1788-1850 [from "Half lights on Chelsfield Court Lodge"- copyright holder unknown]*

PLATE 17 *Alice Dunmall (born 1839) – an unusual cottage interior of 1900 [Mrs. Susannah Bowden]*

PLATE 18 *The only known photograph of the old Goddington House, demolished 1875 [Arthur Waring]*

PLATE 19 *The new Goddington House in its heyday, as remodelled by W. West Neve in the 1890s [Bill Morton]*

PLATE 20 *Norstead Manor House and members of*

the Phillips family, c1875 [Mrs. Eileen Folley]

PLATE 21 *Lilleys Farm in 1912, taken from a watercolour by H.S. Uhlrich [Mrs. Margaret Cobbold]*

Chapter 11

THE MANOR OF CHELSFIELD

" I will in all things demean myself as a faithful tenant ought to do, so help me GOD."

- from the oath of Fealty to be sworn by the Tenants of the Manor of Chelsfield, 1853.

The impression given in history lessons when I was at school was that the Middle Ages, and with them the Manorial System, somehow came to an end with the Battle of Bosworth in 1485, but that is an over-simplification of a complex situation. The power of the Manor had begun to pass away from the time of the scarcity of labour following the Black Death in the middle of the 14th century, a national calamity which had been a blessing in disguise for the manorial tenants who survived. They had for the first time been in a position to bargain for their labour, and had begun the process of commuting the work which they had been bound to do on the Manorial demesne, and in its place to pay an annual rent for their properties, known as a Quitrent.

Because, it seems, no-one in mediaeval times had grasped the facts of inflation, no provision was made to raise these payments. A Quitrent of 2d. per annum for a cottage, 1s.4d. for a smallholding of a few acres like Worlds End, 17s.8d. for a small farm such as Fairtrough, contributing to a total rent roll of some £26 a year for the whole of the Manor of Chelsfield, would have represented a fair income for the Lord in the fourteenth century, but had become negligible even by the beginning of the 18th century. However, in Chelsfield as elsewhere, the Manor continued to operate until well into Victorian times - and in other areas the Manor has persisted into this century.

No documents of any significance have survived for the

Court Lodge 1838, artist unknown (author's collection)

Manor of Chelsfield before 1612, and of the three other Manors based in the parish only Hewitts and Norsted have records from before that. I do not pretend to any knowledge as to how the Manors in this area came to evolve from the pre-Conquest period onwards, and indeed I doubt if anyone could be very specific on this difficult subject. The Lords of some Manors in the mediaeval period exercised legal powers rather similar to those of the later Justices of the Peace, through a Court held at frequent intervals, which was known as the Court Leet or View of Frankpledge. The Lord of the Manor of Chelsfield had no such powers, at least during the period for which records have survived. Chelsfield was one of the parishes or townships over which the Court Leet of the Manor of Farnborough[1] claimed jurisdiction. This important Manor was part of the possessions of the Duchy of Lancaster, but unfortunately few of its records have survived, at least from the earlier period - the wife of an eighteenth century Steward's agent is said to have sold a sack full of ancient rolls and other documents to a paper and glue manufacturer.

The borsholder or parochial representative of Chelsfield, along with those of other nearby parishes including West Wickham, St. Paul's Cray and Keston, had to attend the Court Leet of the Duchy Court. Among the surviving records[2] there is a continuing saga about the Church Green at Chelsfield, which, it was presented in 1697, 1700 and 1707, had been illegally enclosed by Gravely Norton, Lord of the Manor of Chelsfield, and kept enclosed by his son Thomas. Despite being ordered to remove his fences, no effective action was taken, and the land became by virtue of possession part of the Court Lodge estate, and continued as such until quite recently it was acquired by St. Martin's church.

The Manor of Chelsfield was by far the most important in the parish, and covered almost all of Chelsfield and much of Farnborough; it spilled over a little into Shoreham, Halstead and Knockholt, and had some property in Orpington and water meadows in St. Mary Cray. The Demesne of the Manor - that is, the land which went with the Lordship - varied in size from time to time, but it was of considerable extent, and was entirely in Chelsfield parish. Records of Courts Baron which were held for the Manor have survived from 1652 onwards, and Rentals and Rent Rolls from 1612, the whole forming a good series up to 1859, when the last Court was held.

The parchment documents in which the proceedings of the Courts are recorded are known as Court Rolls, and as the Courts by the seventeenth century were held only at intervals of many years, some of the Rolls are of immense length – that for 1717 is over 32 feet long. Some fifty years ago my wife transcribed, and where necessary translated from Latin, all the Court Rolls, but did not have time to deal with all of the other records which were then with the Waring family solicitors, Dimonds, in their Welbeck Street office. Arthur Waring's transcripts of the Court Rolls have disappeared, but by a stroke of good fortune the copies of the Rentals and Rent Rolls which he laboriously transcribed have survived.

The Courts Baron were kept in a very formal way, common to all four Manors in the parish, so it is worth describing this in some detail. The Steward of the Manor, generally a lawyer, presided over the proceedings, which were opened with a proclamation by the Manorial Bailiff, formally calling all the tenants to appear. Next, the excuses of those who had said they would be unable to attend for some good reason were examined, and their names entered under the heading "Essoins". The swearing-in of the Jury (known as the Homage) was the next item: in the earlier period it consisted of 12 Manorial tenants, but the number gradually grew less with the decline in the importance of the Manor itself.

The Homage were charged by the Steward to make true presentments on any matters affecting the rights of the Lord, and first they presented the names of those tenants who had failed to appear or to send an excuse for non-attendance; each defaulter was amerced or fined, usually twelve pence. By the seventeenth century by far the greatest part of the business consisted of keeping a record of changes in ownership of the Manorial properties, whether through death or alienation, whereby a Relief amounting in this Manor to one year's Quitrent became payable to the Lord. The Lord's right to such a payment was challenged at every Court between 1739 and 1828, but Reliefs continued to be exacted. It is from these entries that it is possible to follow the changes in ownership of almost all the properties in the parish, although unfortunately as time went on and the real power of the Manor slipped away, the details given became less reliable.

There are a few entries of more general interest, including references in 1814, 1821 and 1828 to the immemorial custom for the Bailiff to collect a penny from the holder of each booth when Chelsfield Fair was held. In the same years the Homage presented that gravel and turf had been dug illegally at Green Street Green on the Lord's Waste. A fine of 6s.8d. was imposed, although this was a futile gesture since the culprits had not been identified. A similar fine was imposed in 1773 on someone unknown who had lopped a pollard oak on the Waste. In 1814 the Homage presented an encroachment by a Mr. Taylor on Green Street Green by building a cart lodge, and an unnamed couple were presented in 1828 for erecting a hut or tent and a fence on the same Waste of the Lord, and the Bailiff was ordered to pull these down.

In 1717 the Homage presented that the Manorial Pound was

in need of repair – the only reference to this enclosure where cattle were put if found trespassing. Arthur Waring commented in 1912 – "probably many still living in Chelsfield remember the Pound that stood at the end of the shrubbery on the east side of the Church green, and opening into the public road." The Pound is marked on the 1871 six inch Ordnance Survey map, and it would be interesting to know if straying animals were still impounded there after the virtual demise of the Manor in about 1860.

Although the Rentals and Rent Rolls make rather dry reading in general, they contain a vast amount of information which is particularly useful to family historians. The 1674 Rental, for example, is a working copy kept by Gravely Norton, the Lord of the Manor – a daily record of the collection of Quitrents with some interesting additional notes. Two typical entries read – "Thomas and George Wakelyn – Symonds Hawe in Chelsfield – 10s. Received of Joseph King for his part 5s. Received of Henry Langridge who married Tom Wakelin's widow 10s., viz 5s. due from Tom Wakeley in his lifetime for an old arrear And the other 5s was for this Michaelmas 1674. Memo received this 10s. upon Sunday 9th. October 1675 – G. Norton."
"Thomas Allen for one messuage and 20 acres called Washnest in Chelsfield, Thomas Heath tenant – 4s. received of Goodman Heath by the hands of Mr. Skeggs."

The early Lords of the Manor, from the time of the Domesday Book onwards, are recorded in the pages of Hasted, and Arthur Waring expanded considerably on his work, particularly about the de Chelsfield family who were Lords during the twelfth and thirteenth centuries. They were followed by the powerful de Grandisons - Otho de Grandison who died in 1358 is mentioned in the chapter about St. Martin's church before the Reformation, and he and his wife Beatrice are the only Lord and Lady of the Manor from the middle ages who are anything more than mere names to us. Indeed, in their case we even know what they looked like, as they have effigies on their splendid tombs in Ottery St. Mary church, albeit stylised portraits, showing little of Otho's face except his eyes, nose and bushy moustache, because he is wearing his helmet.

Thereafter, the history of the ownership of the Manor is not of great interest until the mid seventeenth century, not least because it seems unlikely that any of the Lords in the intervening period would have been resident in the parish. Among the papers deposited by All Souls College in the Bodleian Library, Oxford, is an abstract of title to the Manor from 1654 to 1753[3], compiled when All Souls were about to buy the Advowson, or the right of presentation to the Rectory of Chelsfield with Farnborough, which had gone with the Lordship of the Manor from time immemorial. By a complicated series of purchases from the owners of shares in the Manor, which had been divided among the six aunts and coheirs of Henry Lee, Thomas Norton of Offley in Essex (who had married one of them) eventually emerged as sole Lord of the Manor in 1657. The path to achieving this had not been a smooth one, and on the way he had had to fight a case in the Court of Chancery, but once he had achieved his goal it would seem that he lived at the Court Lodge until his death not long afterwards.

His son, the curiously named Gravely Norton, succeeded him – his Christian name was his grandmother's surname – and in 1666 he married Anne Hughes of Bromley, when he settled 188 acres of the Demesne land on her. Gravely died in 1693 and was succeeded by his son Thomas Norton, who lived at the Court Lodge for some 56 years, dying aged 80 in 1749. The 1707 Marriage Settlement of this Thomas and his wife Elizabeth Nurse gives an even more detailed list of the lands settled on her, and it is possible without much difficulty to tie up many of the field names with those in the Tithe Map of 1838. Among these are Oxenden Wood, Aspen Spring, Foxberry Wood, Parnells Brooms and Forberry Field, while the house itself came into the settlement, described as "the Court Lodge House together with Dovehouse and Wellhouse".

Thomas Norton, who was probably responsible for the present attractive building, died without children, and in his will[4] he appears as a simple old-fashioned country gentleman, not given to unnecessary show. As to his funeral, he directed "my body to be put into a Good Oake Coffin with a Good thick Lead therein and to be buried in the South Isle in the parish Church of Chelsfield amongst the rest of my Family, and as near my Dear Wife as possible may be and that there be no Escutcheons nor Pall Bearers not the Pulpit Hung with

Mourning and my Body to be carried to the Ground by Six poor men of the said parish to whom I direct Ten shillings apiece to be paid to them for their Trouble and to be attended to the Ground by two or three of my Servants." His unobtrusive wall monument, with carved skull and flaming torches typical of eighteenth century taste, may be seen in St. John's chapel.

He left the Manor with some 414 acres of the Demesne land to Henry Martin, his sister in law's son, who in 1759 sold it to James Maud, a Wine Merchant of Crutched Friars in the City, who also had a country house at Gatton in Surrey. James died in 1769, and when his daughter and only child Mary Tattersall inherited the Manor and came to live in part of the Court Lodge she transferred his belongings from Gatton, as is shown in an Inventory[5] listing many interesting items in detail. These included for example a bedstead with yellow moreen furniture, a five-leaved screen, 8 mahogany chairs with horse-hair seats, a mahogany night stool, many books including the works of Pope, and much silver and linen. A deed of the same year[6] let to Robert Harris most of the Demesne land, and the house except for "the kitchen and parlour at the north end of the house, the two chambers over the same, and the three garrets over the same chambers, the stairs leading to these apartments, the cellar under the said parlour, the large hall, the chamber over the same, the stairs to the said hall, the dining room over the said Robert Harris's kitchen, the free use of the brewhouse and well in the back yard during the said term in common with the said Robert Harris, the court yard and Church Green in front of the said house, the two coach houses and stables in the said court yard ..." and some small fields and gardens around the house, which were also reserved to Mary Tattersall's use. Another clause gave the Lady of the Manor "power liberty and authority to hold and keep the Court Leet and Court Baron or either of them belonging to the Manor of Chelsfield" as often as she should think fit. Robert Harris, on reasonable notice, was bound "to provide convenient stable room and litter for the horses of such number of persons as shall repair and come to every such Court, also stable room and litter for the horses of the Lady of the Manor, or her Bailiff." After Mary married Brass Crosby in 1771 they lived for six months of the year at the Court Lodge and the remainder at her husband's house in London. Alderman Crosby, Lord Mayor of London and champion of the liberty of the press, was perhaps the most celebrated inhabitant of Chelsfield, to whose memory, on the initiative of the Chelsfield Village Society, a blue plaque has recently been erected in Church Road.

When I was doing my National Service in the RAF in 1949 I was stationed at West Kirby, and discovered the fine Picton Hall Library in nearby Liverpool. Then as now my first thought was to look under Chelsfield in the topographical index, and to my surprise I found a little privately-printed volume, produced in 1933, called "Half lights on Chelsfield Court Lodge." It had been presented to that Library because the author, Alexander Theodore Brown (who shyly hid under his initials) was a citizen of Liverpool. He was a descendant of the Morland and Crawford families who had lived at the Court Lodge from the death of Brass Crosby's widow in 1800 until 1844.

There are fascinating extracts from correspondence, and portraits of several of the people concerned, including two Lords of the Manor – George Morland (died 1814) and Robert Crawford. Altogether the book is both fascinating and tantalising, because it is clear that, despite the destruction of some family papers which Mr. Brown deplored, he still had access to many, which would be of the greatest interest to me – if they still exist and could be traced.

The Crawford family were strongly attached to the Court Lodge, but Robert is described by Mr. Brown as "a sorry farmer" and eventually he had to sell the house, the Manor and the estate. It was put up for auction at Garraway's Coffee House in London on 24 July 1844, when the description in the Maidstone Journal painted the property in glowing colours. The house must have become somewhat run-down, as potential buyers were assured that it would be "improveable at a trifling expense." A selling point was that "the intended Railway from Croydon through Bromley to the Crays will go within three miles of this Estate", which is described as being in a good state of cultivation, and abounding with game. The auction must have been an event of much interest for the local inhabitants, and we know from his journal that it was attended by Samuel Brooker of Lilleys.

Unfortunately, however, the estate failed to sell at that time, which must have been a severe blow for the beleaguered Robert Crawford. It was not until some months later that the property, together with the Lordship of the Manor, was bought by Thomas Waring, crowning his career in building up his estate in the parish. In 1836 Thomas had been portrayed by Abraham Cooper RA in a fine oil painting (also produced as an engraving) entitled "Thomas Waring Esquire on his horse Peter with six couple of his harriers." It shows the elderly but still vigorous Thomas clad in green, in the fields to the east of Woodlands; in the background is the White Cottage at Well Hill where his huntsman lived, and there is a distant view of Shooters Hill. Thomas died at Woodlands in 1852, and all his estate, and the Lordships of Chelsfield and Hewitts, descended to his only surviving son William Waring, as recounted in the chapter about the latter.

In the Tithe map of Chelsfield, surveyed in 1838, a huge range of farm buildings is shown to the east of the Court Lodge, and it had puzzled me why these why these did not appear in the 25" Ordnance Survey of 1868, until I found this item in the South Eastern Gazette for 28 July 1857:

"Dreadful fire at Chelsfield Court Lodge - about 2 o'clock in the morning of Thursday last, a fire broke out among the extensive farm buildings occupied by Mr. B. Spain. Owing to the long drought, so furiously did the fire rage, that the whole of the buildings were speedily on fire. There is little doubt that some vile incendiary is the cause of the serious calamity, and in fact suspicion rests on someone... [in the early morning] Wickenden, a ploughman employed on the farm, was disturbed in his slumber by the smell of smoke, and very soon discovered that a fire had broken out in one of his master's barns. He exerted himself manfully in releasing the stock and spreading alarm, but it was soon evident that the mass of buildings and their contents would fall a prey to the flames, and building after building ignited.... The buildings destroyed consisted of 3 large barns, a granary, several sheds, a cow-house, stabling, and pigstyes, the whole covering a space of nearly an acre in extent..."

The Bartholomew Spain mentioned in this report was the last tenant farmer to live in the Court Lodge; when he retired, in the early sixties, the opportunity was taken to build the present Court Lodge Farm for future tenant farmers, and to begin to let the Court Lodge and a few surrounding acres of land to a succession of well-heeled tenants. The second of these, who lived there with his family from about 1874, was Frederick William Brind, a prosperous wine merchant. In 1880 his daughter Marian Harriet Brind was married at Chelsfield to the eminent artist Randolph Caldecott, who was well-known for his work as an illustrator, chiefly of books for children, a number of which, notably "The three jovial huntsmen", are set in Chelsfield, with the Court Lodge prominently featured. Of even greater interest locally is a little volume called "The owls of O'lynn belfry," privately published in about 1885, because it features a number of local inhabitants; they can be identified because quite recently a copy of the book, with the names of the people added, came to light in Chelsfield vestry. This discovery caused great interest among members of the Randolph Caldecott Societies in this country and the United States, because it includes the first positive identification of Marian, of whom no known photograph has survived. Her father, sister Maggie and brother Frank also appear in several of the drawings.

After the Brinds gave up the Court Lodge in about 1893, it was let to another wealthy London merchant, George Edward Asprey, and his second wife Florence Caroline Rolls; he became Chairman of the family firm of Aspreys the Bond Street jewellers in 1909. Three tragic events occurred during their occupancy; their young daughter Joan Rolls Asprey died in 1907, and is commemorated in stained glass in the Norman window at the west end of the church, while their son Maurice, a Captain in the Buffs, was killed in action in 1916. Finally, two years later there was another fire at the Court Lodge which, in the words of the reporter of the Kentish Times, "began in the kitchen of the groom, Mr. Pettit, who was chauffeur to Mr. Asprey. Mr. Pettit... retired to bed about half past ten on Friday and was awakened by a strong smell of smoke. On opening his bedroom door he found the stairs were burning fiercely and his means of escape that way cut off. Quickly snatching a pair of sheets from the bed, he tied them together... and lowered himself to the ground from the window" when his first thought was to remove the cars from the garage.

Mr. Asprey meanwhile appeared and helped him, but "suddenly collapsed, and expired before medical aid could be forthcoming." The Aspreys like the Brinds and the Crawfords before them had become very fond of the Court Lodge, and this was a sad end to their connection with Chelsfield, Mrs. Asprey moving from the parish not long afterwards.

To turn again from the people who lived in the Court Lodge to the history of the final stages of the Manor in Chelsfield, William Waring was nothing if not practical, and on coming into his inheritance it would seem that he soon decided that although the days of the manorial system in the parish were numbered, it might be possible to squeeze a fair amount of cash out of the dying process, to which end, initially, a Court Baron was called for the Manor of Chelsfield in 1853. Evidently with this event in mind, the Steward began a Minute Book in which he noted the traditional forms of the various Proclamations and oaths. The Proclamation read – "Oyez oyez oyez ! All manner of persons who owe suit and service to William Waring Esquire Lord of this Manor now to be holden or who have been summoned to appear at this time and place draw near and give your attendance every man answering to his name when called and thereby saving his amercement." Even at this late date the oath administered by the Steward was worded in abject terms – "You swear to become a true and faithful tenant to William Waring Esquire Lord of this Manor for the Estate to which you made your acknowledgement of tenure at this Court, you shall from time to time bear pay and perform all such rents duties services and customs in respect of the same estate as are due and of right accustomed; you shall from time to time be ordered and justified in all things at the Lord's Court to be holden in and for this Manor as other the tenants of this Manor are shall or ought to be and you shall in all things demean yourself as a faithful tenant ought to do, so help you GOD."

Despite the intimidating tone of the summons from the Steward (Mr. Waring's solicitor John Simpson, of Simpson and Dimond) threatening that "a distress will speedily be taken on your Lands and Tenements, if you shall neglect this Summons," it seems that few took the trouble to attend, and the Homage on that occasion consisted of only two tenants,

William Morgan and William Hills. Again in the time-honoured way, all defaulting tenants were amerced one shilling, but it seems highly unlikely that these fines were enforced.

A few presentments were made as to changes in ownership, and the Steward drew up a final Rental, or detailed list of all the freeholders, the Manorial names of the properties they held and the annual Quitrents payable. This was the prelude to the Steward pursuing all those who had failed to respond to the summons, demanding the payment of Quitrents and all arrears; in a curious mixture of the mediaeval and the modern he wrote: "...we request that you will oblige us with a Post Office order for the amount payable at the Office in Old Cavendish Street." William Waring himself collected some of the Quitrents and wrote to his solicitor giving him the details, adding in a characteristic postscript - "the sooner you communicate with all those defaulters we arranged you should - the better."

There is no record of how successful these efforts were overall, but a fair proportion of the Quitrents and arrears must have been paid at that time; it is interesting that, generally speaking, it would seem to have been easier to collect these from the upper class tenants. This I think was not because they were better off, but because they were anxious to maintain the existing order - particularly those such as Sir Percyvall Hart Dyke of Lullingstone and Mr. Atkins of Halstead, who were Lords of Manors themselves. Indeed, Sir Percyvall's solicitor's accounts[7] show that, as late as 1867, Mr. Waring was entertained at Lullingstone Castle where the subject of a possible "exchange of Quitrents" was discussed, with what result is unknown; this was one of those occasions when I would dearly have liked to have heard the exchanges which passed between them.

In 1859 the final Court Baron for the Manor of Chelsfield was held, with a somewhat larger attendance, and a Homage of 6 freeholders, whose names were - William Hills the Postmaster, freeholder of the Post Office, Worlds End and other properties; John Graves, freeholder of Sluts Hole and Codling Cottages; John Cope, freeholder of a cottage at Pratts Bottom which his ancestor had been allowed to build on the Manorial Waste; Thomas Blundell, freeholder of Yew Tree Cottage at Maypole;

Richard Hickmott, freeholder of property at Pratts Bottom, and also of the Bull's Head which was in the Manor of Hewitts; and William Morgan, the freeholder of the cottage next to the Five Bells, later known as Brynterion, another property which had originally been erected by leave of the Lord on the Waste of the Manor.

Following the holding of this Court there ensued some spirited correspondence between the Steward and those tenants who had refused to pay up - notably with Joseph Snelling of St. Mary Cray. After several exchanges, Mr. Snelling lost patience and wrote tartly to Simpson and Dimond: "...all I can say is, I shall feel greatly obliged to you if you can prove my right to any portion of land that ever belonged to the late Sir Thomas Dyke purchased as you state by my father in 1828..." This prompted another letter from William Waring to Mr. Simpson - "I think there is no alternative but to give up the claims for Quit Rents on Messrs. T.H. Smith and Snelling. I have not received any of the Quit Rents, but I will speak to the Overseers and Church Wardens of Chelsfield, and I have no doubt they will then pay me. I will also manage Mr. Crowther - as I have a small settling with him - and most probably you might write to him to all eternity, without getting any answer, as he is far removed from "the upper 10,000..." I think it would be well to send a reminder to the others..."

The scene was now set for the final act in the drama. It was possible to extinguish all future claims on manorial properties by a single payment, and Mr. Waring was able to persuade a number of the manorial freeholders to part with quite substantial amounts in order to do this. Again, it is remarkable that it was members of the upper classes who were more open to persuasion in this respect - for example George Warde Norman, at one time Governor of the Bank of England, the freeholder of Chelsfield Hall Farm. He was persuaded to part with no less than £27.15s.4d. in order to extinguish Quitrents of 7s.2d. and 2s.8d. per annum payable for his holdings, as a most impressive document[8] now with the title deeds of Chelsfield Hall confirms.

I believe that most of the manorial tenants, aware that the Manor was by then almost a spent force, resisted all blandishments to pay out in this way. In theory, therefore,

Quitrents remained payable on most property in Chelsfield, a fact which is acknowledged in a number of Sales particulars at least up to the end of the 19th. century. I think however that William Waring could be well pleased with his efforts, and the largely honorific title of Lord of the Manor still counted for something in his lifetime and indeed in those of his son Arthur Thomas and his grandson William Arthur Waring of Hewitts, the last resident Lord who died in 1945 - even if on the debit side it did mean having to head the list of subscribers to every worthy fund in the parish.

Chelsfield Village from the Recreation Ground.
Drawing by Frank Tilbury, 1951

References

1 See papers by Maurice Bond in Arch. Cant. volumes LVII and LIX.
2 CKS, U1205/M5.
3 Bodleian Library Oxford, DD C12/5.
4 PCC, PROB 11/770.
5 CKS, U1592/E17.
6 CKS, U291/T2-4.
7 CKS, U806/E19.
8 CKS, U310/T14.

Chapter 12

THE MANOR OF GODDINGTON

"A Distress will speedily be taken upon your Lands and Tenements, if you shall neglect this Summons..."

-from a printed form commanding a tenant to attend the Court Baron of Goddington, 1782.

I believe that nothing based on original research has been published about this small Manor since Hasted wrote his monumental History of Kent, which began publication in 1778. His account of the ownership of the Manor by the De Godynton family in the middle ages, and subsequent changes down to his own day, seems to have been quoted without question in all subsequent published works on Chelsfield and district. I have done no research on the Manor before the seventeenth century, and although I have no reason to doubt the accuracy of what Hasted wrote about the early period, there is no point in repeating the story yet again. Rather will I try to put some flesh on the bare bones of the period from 1636 to 1931, based on research in a variety of documents.

Goddington Manor House is at the extreme northern tip of the ancient parish of Chelsfield, and the Demesne lands (that is, the lands owned personally by the Lord) extended to some 236 acres within it. However, a study of the three remaining Court Rolls[1] shows that, with one exception, the Manor properties (that is, the houses and lands which were held by Manorial tenants) were all in Orpington or St. Mary Cray.

The first surviving Court Roll dates from 1636 when the Lord of the Manor was Alexander Haddon, presumably then a minor since the Court was held by his Guardian, Thomas Lord. Alexander held the next Court personally, in 1663. The third Court Roll to have come down to us dates from 1706, by which time the Manor had been acquired by the ambitious James Styles of Lilleys.

In the chapter about the Manor of Chelsfield I have explained how such Courts were held, and the system was exactly the same in the Manor of Goddington. The Quitrents payable by the tenants here were mostly very small, and the Lord did not have the right to claim the occasional Heriot which made some Manors so profitable. He was entitled only to a Relief on death or alienation, amounting to one third of the Quitrent, so it is perhaps surprising that the feudal trappings were maintained at Goddington. Perhaps it was to do with the social cachet conferred by being the Lord or Lady of a Manor – something for which people are prepared to pay, even today.

We know that a Court was held here as late as 1782, as a summons to Thomas Fuller to attend it in that year survived in the Waring MSS. This referred to the Quitrent of 3d. having remained unpaid for 39 years, and uttered a menacing warning to dispossess the tenant if he should neglect to appear. Both Lord and tenant must have known that this was an empty threat, but all the same Thomas duly paid up: 9s.9d. for arrears of Quitrent, 4d. for Acquittance and 3s.6d. for miscellaneous charges summarised as Relief, Presentment, Entry and Cryer. I have not so far found any evidence of Courts being kept up later than this date.

Among the Manorial properties were a messuage called "le Red Lyon" and 3 other messuages and gardens adjoining in St. Mary Cray, Quitrent two shillings, a messuage and garden called the Bull in Orpington (threepence) and 6 acres called the Brooks in St. Mary Cray (sixpence). The mention of the only property in Chelsfield comes as a surprise – no less than "a messuage called the Courtlodge" which was said to have been held by the largest Quitrent on the roll, 7s.9d. per annum. How it should have come about that a tiny Manor like Goddington claimed that the Manor House of the powerful Manor of Chelsfield owed it allegiance is a mystery to me, and it would be interesting to know if the Quitrent was in fact paid. It is all the more puzzling since the Lord of Chelsfield claimed a Quitrent of £1.3s.1d. from Goddington, as shown in the Rentals of 1652 and 1674 of that Manor.

Goddington was one of the properties involved in the great Chelsfield inheritance case of 1729-1733, as described in another chapter. In the seminal division of the valuable disputed estate according to the law of Gavelkind[2], "all that the Manor or Lordship of Goddington with the right members and appurtenances thereof and the farm called Goddington ...in the occupation of James Burton" was awarded to Susan Vice and Mary Aynscomb, and counted as one third of the whole. They were entitled to this as being "the only daughters and heirs of James Cox late of Nutfield Surrey yeoman deceased, who was the only son and heir of Sarah Cox, one of the three great aunts of John Styles deceased." It would seem that Susan parted with her half to her sister Mary Aynscomb who thus became sole owner and Lady of the Manor. When she died in 1755 she left Goddington to two of her sons, James and Anthony, and the latter sold his share to James in about 1765.

James Aynscomb lived at Goddington for the rest of his life, and evidently interested himself in improving the estate. In 1773 he must have spent a considerable sum in diverting part of Goddington Lane[3] so that it came nearer to his house – not something which a landowner would generally find desirable these days. In order to do so he had to obtain the consent of two local Justices of the Peace, Andrew de Visme and George Greenwood, the Vestry meeting and also the leading inhabitants of Chelsfield. In a document dated 1 January 1773 thirteen of them, headed by Charles Meetkerke the Rector, Brass Crosby the Lord of the Manor and James Rondeau of Hewitts, agreed that James might:

"divert and turn the present Highway leading from Orpington Gravel Pits towards Chelsfield by opening and making at his own expense a good sufficient carriage way twenty feet wide at least in all parts from the extremity of the lands of Sir John Dixon Dyke Bart. in the occupation of Elizabeth Seddon widow on the south side of the said Highway upon a straight line towards the north east through certain lands belonging to the said James Aynscomb called Haggetts to a clump of elm trees in the hedge next adjoining and from thence into Goddington Lane being in length 80 rods [444 yards] or thereabouts," and in return for this he was to take the site of the old road to his own use. James undertook to make "with all convenient speed such good and sufficient carriage way twenty feet wide at the least in all parts for the space aforesaid through his aforesaid lands."

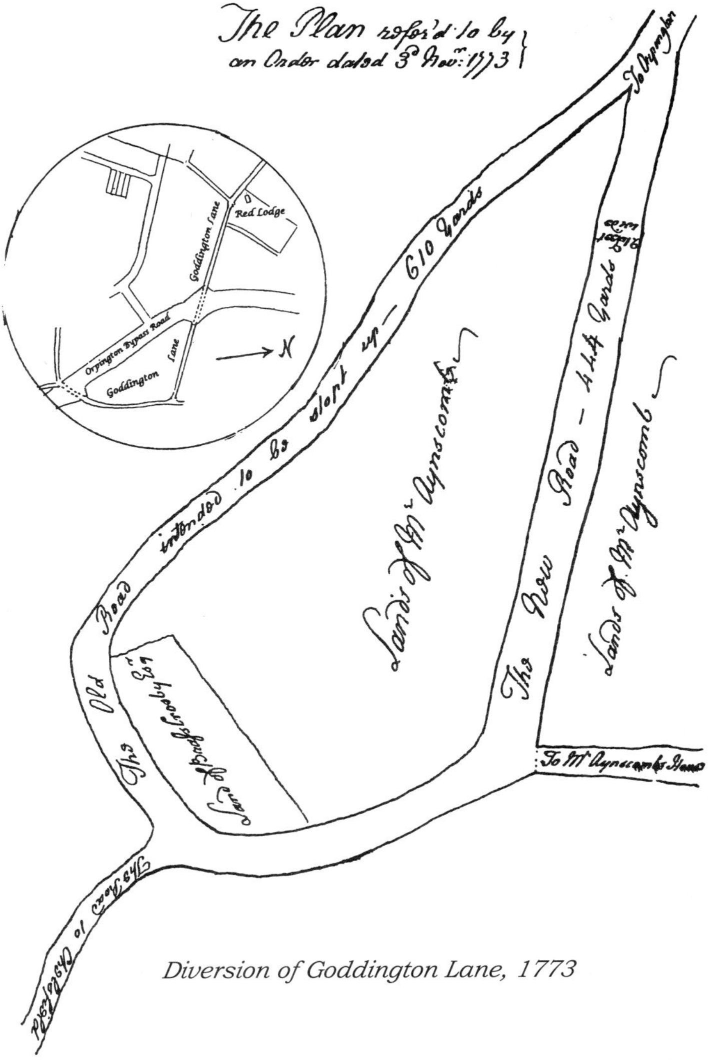

Diversion of Goddington Lane, 1773

After the new road was completed it would "for ever afterwards be accounted a Parish Highway" and the Justices authorised a rate not exceeding 6d. in the pound to be charged on property owners in the parish to compensate James for the land occupied by the new road and for making any necessary ditches and fences. The rather rough map attached to the documents shows the position of the new road, which stands out, even today, as being the only straight section of Goddington Lane, although it was unfortunately cut through when Court Road (the Orpington Bypass) was built in the 1920s.

James would seem to have got quite a good bargain through this transaction, but it would appear that some years later he was in need of ready cash, since he borrowed £700 from George Mace, the landlord of the Five Bells. There are records[4] of the payment of £31.10s.0d. annual interest from 1780 to 1783, when James died, and after his death his widow Mary paid off the principal in several instalments. Interestingly, in 1786 she also paid £20.4s.0d. "for a Note of Hand given by my late husband James Aynscomb to Mrs. Elizabeth Colchin about 20 years ago, which said Note is either lost or mislaid.[5]"

James and Mary Aynscomb had only one child, Mary, who was the heiress to both Goddington and Lilleys, and she was soon snapped up. At the age of 17 in 1787, with the consent of her "natural and lawful mother", she was married at Chelsfield to the 21 year old James Harris. He came from Erith, and no doubt would have met Mary because he was the nephew of Robert Harris, the tenant of the Court Lodge lands.

When Mary Aynscomb made her will[6] in the same year she left her property in a complex trust for the benefit of her daughter Mary Harris for life; upon whose death all was to be divided equally among the latter's surviving children, whether male or female, a provision which, much later, led to legal complications. Mary Aynscomb died in 1793 and James and Mary Harris lived at Goddington for the rest of their lives, James farming the land himself for many years.

In April 1835 James, then aged 69, made his will[7]. His large estate had come to him through his wife – this was long before the Married Women's Property Act – and consisted of Goddington, Lilleys and houses and land in Orpington, and he left it to her for life, then to be divided equally among his three sons and one daughter. In July 1835 the daughter, Maria, was married at Lewisham to William Cole, a builder from Keston. The following month her father added a codicil to his will – "whereas my daughter Maria Harris now Maria Cole has since the date of my will married against my wishes Now I hereby revoke the bequest in favour of all my children, it being my intention that Maria shall not take any part of my said real and personal estate so I give it equally to my 3 sons..."

Maria was then aged 41, but presumably father did not like the idea of her marrying out of her class. In fact, James did not cut his daughter off completely, since she was made a rather stingy allowance of £40 per annum for life.

James died in 1837, and his widow in 1846. Her funeral was entrusted to Henry French, the Chelsfield village carpenter and undertaker, who lived at Bucks Cross, and his account, for no less that £44.14s.0d., has survived[8]. It includes items such as "A Stout Elm Shell Lin'd frilled and prepared for leading Mattress and Pillow etc. - £2.15s.0d.: A Stout Oak Coffin Covered with Best Black Cloth and full furnished - £7.15s.0d.: Silk Scarf band and Gloves for 2 Clergymen - £4." Because she was laid to rest in one of the Harris vaults, there are two items "To attendance and asisting the Plummer – 10s.: to Attendance floor laid over the Vault - £2.10s."

The funeral once observed with due solemnity, it was now time for the three sons and coheirs to think about what was to be done, both to divide the property among them, and to satisfy the claims of their sister, to whom I am sure they were not unkindly disposed. The difficulty, of course, was that whatever her father might have wished, Maria was unquestionably entitled to one fourth part of the Goddington estate left by her grandmother Mary Aynscomb over 50 years before, and there are two huge documents which are concerned with this problem[9]. In a deed dated 15 March 1847 the three brothers agreed to pay Maria a lump sum of £1000, and to continue paying the £40 annuity given to her by her father, for life. In return, Maria and her husband agreed to convey any interest they might have in the property left by her grandmother, to the three brothers.

This deed was duly executed, and in another very large document is a record of the agreement reached by the brothers on 10 May 1847, setting out the property which each was to receive. For this purpose, all the landed property left by James Harris was valued by Francis Fuller and Thomas Stow, who were "nominated by the parties to make a fair and just valuation of the three shares so that any necessary adjustment may be made between the parties." Robert Allen was also called in to value the "timber trees tellers and saplings down to the value of one shilling per stick then growing upon the Estates."

By far the highest valuation, at £7303, was that of "the Manor of Goddington alias Goldington" and the lands belonging to it, and this was awarded to James Aynscomb, the eldest son: Lilleys Farm and lands were valued at £5278.6s.0d, and awarded to John Harris, the second son, while the lands in Orpington were valued at £6124.6s.6d. and awarded to George St. Pierre Harris, the youngest son. To make the division fair, James Aynscomb Harris made the necessary financial adjustments with his brothers, and thus he became the owner of the Goddington estate[10].

Goddington continued in the ownership of the Harris family until in 1871, for reasons which are not clear, it was sold by James Aynscomb Harris's son Harry George Minshaw Harris, ending a family connection with the estate of some 170 years. The catalogue[11] of "all the valuable live and dead farming stock" sold by auction on 5 April 1871 goes into great detail, even including the names of the horses – among them two powerful and active grey draught horses called Dumpling and Colonel, two bay mares called Jewel and Blossom and a chestnut bay horse called Punch. Among the dead stock were a set of bells for four horses, six waggons, turn-wrest and other ploughs and a two-horse thrashing machine.

After being briefly in the ownership of the Hohler family Goddington became the property of George Hallett, a very wealthy London businessman, whose interests were not in the City but in Rotherhithe. He it was who first began to dignify Goddington with the name "Goddington Hall", and when he died there in 1873 his effects were sworn at "under £140,000". His wife Marianne died shortly afterwards, and they both lie in Chelsfield churchyard, under a tomb to the south of the chancel. Under the provisions of George's will, Goddington descended to his sister Emily Caroline Hallett.

In Miss Hallett's will dated 1890 she described herself as "spinster and gentlewoman" of Goddington Hall, but she also had a house in Campden Hill, Middlesex. Among numerous bequests to friends and servants, £50 was left "to George

French who for many years acted as the Foreman of the Works connected with the business some time ago carried on by me at Rotherhithe, to buy some article as a memento of me."
Evidently she had pursued her brother's business with some success, because when she died in April 1892 her effects were sworn at over £161,000, an enormous amount for the period. The principal beneficiary was her nephew Alexander Miller-Hallett, to whom she had given the Goddington estate three months before her death, and with his ownership began the brief, golden period in its history.

Mr. Miller-Hallett was born plain Alexander Miller, the elder son of Robert Miller, a London physician, and his wife Elizabeth Ann Tamplin. I think that the younger son Robert must also have been fortunate in inheriting a fortune from a relative since (as shown in their father's will) both added to their surnames: while Alexander became Miller-Hallett, Robert became Tamplin-Miller.

Alexander must have been made aware of his expectation of inheriting Goddington, because at the sale of the Mayfield estate in 1888[12] he made the astute move of purchasing Gravelpit Farm, Orpington. This consisted of farm buildings and cottages (on the site of the present junction of Spur Road and Sevenoaks Road) and 130 acres abutting on the lands belonging to Goddington.

Mr. Miller-Hallett, who was another London businessman with the unusual occupation of antimony refiner, took up residence at Goddington, and it is clear from numerous references in the early Parish Magazines that he relished his entry into rural life. In 1895, for example -

"...the Church Sunday School Treat was held on January 18th.; a capital tea was provided, and after the prizes, certificates, and toys had been distributed, Mr. Miller-Hallett exhibited to the delighted children a most excellent series of dissolving views..."

"A General Meeting of the Cricket Club was held on Tuesday, 19th. November, at which Mr. Miller-Hallett took the chair... Hearty votes of thanks were passed to Messrs. Norman, Miller-Hallett and Asprey (Captain) for the great interest they have taken in the welfare of the Club..."

Cricket was an abiding interest, and grand matches were

staged at Goddington. In Sir David Waldron Smithers' book on Knockholt I came across a reference to Mr. Miller-Hallett's ladies' cricket team, but I know nothing further about that.

One of the first things Mr. Miller-Hallett did on arriving in the parish was to give the present organ to St. Martin's church, and to contribute substantially to the cost of building a new vestry to accommodate it. This was a long saga with a happy outcome, about which I have written elsewhere[13].

So far as I am aware, there is no record of the ancient mansion which must have existed at Goddington. Arthur Waring included a photograph of a later house in his Parochial Notes but did not mention where he got it from, or when it was taken. The house pictured looks like a large mid-nineteenth century villa, but it may well be that it was a much older building with a Victorian façade. In the 1931 sale particulars a rather ambiguous description of Goddington refers to the house being "dated August 1875," and the 1919 sale particulars state that "the handsome modern mansion was remodelled and enlarged regardless of cost by the present owner for his own occupation, under the supervision of a well-known London Architect (a pupil of Norman Shaw) about 25 years since..."

The architect in question was William West Neve, who had also been employed to design the new Vestry. He came originally from Cranbrook, and did not rely on his architectural practice for a living, as he enjoyed a large private income. Andrew Saint in his biography of Shaw unkindly dismisses Neve as "not clever except as a conjuror," but I find Goddington an attractive building, very much in the Norman Shaw tradition.

Mr. Miller-Hallett further improved the estate by the skilful planting of trees both in the park immediately around the house, and in the southern part of the former Gravelpit Farm lands. It was through the latter that the carriage drive (now Park Avenue) wound its way to the Sevenoaks Road. Three picturesque lodges, and the commodious house known as Red Lodge in Goddington Lane, together with motor houses (as garages were originally known), farm buildings and a cricket pavilion were all built in this period. The 1901 Census returns show that, although the Miller-Halletts were not in residence at the time, the staff included a footman, a butler, a cook, three housemaids, a kitchen maid and a scullery maid. There were also a gardener, a farm bailiff, a dairy maid, a coachman, two grooms, an electrical engineer, a waggoner, a cattleman, a gamekeeper, a laundress and a laundry maid. The estate was at the peak of perfection when disaster struck with the outbreak of war in 1914.

Alexander and Amy Miller-Hallett had six children, of whom Stewart Alexander, a Second Lieutenant in the South Wales Borderers, was killed at Mametz Wood in July 1916. Not only did his parents have this personal loss, shared with so many other families in the parish, but the war led to the end of the days of gracious living at Goddington. On 15 July 1919 the whole of the "highly important and very valuable freehold residential estate" with over 370 acres in Chelsfield and Orpington was put up for auction in London, split into 3 lots. It was a difficult time for trying to sell such properties, when landowners everywhere who had been hard hit by wartime taxation and changed social conditions were struggling to trim their expenses.

The sale particulars for Goddington were luxuriously produced, and it was obviously hoped at that time that at least the mansion, farm buildings, Red Lodge and nearly 175 acres of surrounding park would be sold as a going concern rather than for development. In the event, very little if any of the property sold at the auction, and the situation was further complicated by the Orpington Bypass being driven through the estate in the mid twenties.

In 1929 a further auction took place, and the particulars show that by then only about 45 acres had been sold. This time the sights were not set so high, and suggested uses for the mansion were as a golf, country or sports club. The fine photographs of the interior show that it was then empty, while the land was split into 13 lots, promoted as being suitable for building. Evidently this auction was rather more successful, but still the mansion and some 140 acres surrounding it remained unsold, divided into 14 lots for a third auction in 1931. It was suggested this time that the mansion would be well suited for conversion into a residential hotel, a country club or a school, and a map showing a possible layout for developing the park surrounding it was included. Lots 1 and 2, the house, outbuildings, walled kitchen gardens, six "good cottages" and over 12 acres of land had "an absurdly low upset price of £5,500," which seems fair comment.

I believe that it was at or soon after this sale that the bulk of the land came into the ownership of the local Council, a far-sighted and indeed rather unusual action for the period, and it has remained a public open space to this day. The house was purchased separately and remained in residential use.

Although Arthur Waring added a little to the early history of the Manor in his notes, here as with other properties which he did not own himself he evidently felt that it would not be the thing for one gentleman to ask another if he could see his title deeds – although I am sure that Mr. Miller-Hallett would have been delighted to help. I have not so far been able to discover if any of these deeds have survived; if they have, they would indeed be of great interest.

Amy Miller-Hallett died in 1932 and was buried at Chelsfield, when her abode was given as Shortlands, Bromley. Alexander Miller-Hallett survived her by over 30 years, dying at Rottingdean in Sussex in 1953, aged 97. Although he was still relatively wealthy, in his later years he must surely have looked back with nostalgia and regret to the halcyon pre-1914 days at Goddington.

<u>References</u>

1 CKS reference U71/M10.

2 Harris MSS A32.

3 Harris MSS B68-70.

4 Harris MSS B71.

5 Harris MSS B72..

6 PCC, PROB11/1237.

7 PCC, PROB11/1899.

8 Harris MSS A48.

9 Harris MSS A49/50.

10 The account of the descent of Goddington in the eighteenth and nineteenth centuries in "The book of Orpington" is inaccurate.

11 CKS, U2725/B2/327.

12 British Library, Maps 137 c 6 (11).

13 See "Alexander Miller-Hallett and the presentation of the new organ to Chelsfield Church," typescript in Bromley Local Studies Library.

Chapter 13

THE MANOR OF NORSTEAD

"The close proximity of the Property to the Metropolis...renders it exceedingly valuable as a Residential Estate for a Gentleman engaged in Business and fond of Pleasure Farming..."

- from the sale particulars of Northstead [sic] Manor Farm, 1879

As with the other Manors, I am not concerned here with the earliest period, but researches from the sixteenth century onwards have enabled me to supplement the account given in the pages of Hasted. An indenture of 1561[1] shows that in that year Thomas Heneage of the City of London Esquire and Ann his wife conveyed "all that their Manor of Northested in Chelsfield, Farnborough and Cudham," which they had bought from William Fox of London, Goldsmith two years before, to John Lennard of Chevening Esquire, for £640.

John Lennard later became the tenant of the great house of Knole at Sevenoaks, and in a deed of 1587[2] he let to Nycholas Cawston of West Wickham yeoman for 12 years "all that his great messuage or farmhouse of the Manor of Northested and lands in Chelsfield and Cudham, reserving to himself and his heirs the Manor and Royalty and all rents and services, hawking, hunting and game of pheasants, partridges and herons breeding within the said Manor..."

For this Nycholas was to pay £45 and also twenty dozen of conies [rabbits] yearly, one dozen weekly after Midsummer until the total of twenty dozen was reached, to be delivered at Knole "fayer kylled and strete caryed and brought thyther" as the original graphically puts it. There is much else of interest in the lease, which shows that rabbits were a very important feature of this part of the parish.

An endorsement to the deed confirms that on 30 October 1594 Samson Lennard of Knole, John Lennard's son and heir, allowed the remaining term of the lease to be taken over by Persevale Smale of Halstead. Persevale was to be permitted to let certain of the lands but he or his heirs were to inhabit the "mansion house" and occupy the grounds nearby. Killing the rabbits and carrying them to Knole must have been a nuisance, and the endorsement notes that for the future this would be commuted in lieu of an additional rent of £4 per annum.

In 1638, the date of another lease in the same collection, John Skeggs of Chelsfield, gentleman, let to Richard Jewell, son of John Jewell of Oxted in Surrey, yeoman, the Manor house and lands containing by estimation 500 acres more or less, in Chelsfield and Cudham; the rent had rocketed to £80 per annum.

John Skeggs reserved the liberty to keep the Court Baron in the Manor House, and also "all Rents, Services, Wards, Marriages and Reliefs due to the said Manor." For his part, Richard Jewell was in effect to be the agent of the Manor, and "to yearly collect the Quit Rents, Reliefs, Heriots and all other services due to the Manor of Northstead" and to pay them to John Skeggs. John would allow him ten shillings to "find and provide to the Lord of the Manor of Northstead and his Steward, Surveyor or other officers of the Manor and their servants and for the Jury or Homage there appearing once every year a good and sufficient dinner and meat for their horses" when the Court Baron was held.

The Manor itself was a subsidiary of the Manor of Chelsfield, from which it was held by annual Quitrent of £1.8s.0d. The few records of Norstead Manor which have survived begin with some scrappy notes from Elizabethan times. These start in 1559[3] and consist of extracts only, which were evidently put together for some unknown legal purpose in about 1750, possibly to demonstrate what rights the Lord should enjoy. Among these were the Heriot, the best beast belonging to the tenant, claimed on each death or alienation; if there were no beast, then a dead Heriot of only 3s.6d. was payable.

Among the "best beasts" which were successfully claimed by the Lord were "a Cowe colour pied" in 1600, a horse value 40s.

(1611) and a roan coloured spayed beast sold back for 35s. (1617). 1736 was a particularly good year for the Lord, Thomas Skeggs, gentleman, as he claimed from the heirs of the great Chelsfield inheritance case (see that chapter) three Heriots when they sold some of the Chelsfield Hall lands to Charles Polhill – a blackball faced horse (£12), a cow (£3) and a black gelding (£10). Not only that, but two black coach geldings value £10 each were claimed in respect of lands called Mace croft, Oakmer field, Mabb Croft, Shepherds Haw and All Hawes field.

Norstead was one of those Manors in which some of the Quitrents were paid in eggs, hens and cocks. Rames in Farnborough, for example, identifiable as Ramus Wood at Green Street Green, was held by Quitrent of 8d. and 15 hens per annum. Complications arose if a holding with a rent of this type should be split between heirs. The proceedings at the Court held in 1617 are a goldmine for family historians, outlining the complex relationships of members of the Spackman, Dalton, Harman and Collyns alias Goulding families, and at their request apportioning the Quitrents to be paid for various properties. One of them, Allhawes, was assessed at 4d. and half a hen per annum.

Such records of this Manor as we have are confusing, and the Court held in 1736 was the last one of which an account has survived. Although the total of the Quitrents payable amounted to little more than £2 per annum, the windfalls of live Heriots must have been a strong inducement to the Lords to keep the Manor going for as long as they could.

The history of how the Skeggs family came to be Lords of this Manor as given by Hasted is not entirely accurate. He states that at the beginning of the reign of James I [reigned 1603-25] Henry Lennard, Lord Dacre conveyed it to Lady Wolrich, but that is a simplification of the situation. In fact, it would seem that the Manor and lands were sold to Edward Skeggs, a wealthy Haberdasher of London whose family originated in Huntingdonshire. In his will[4] of 1608 he left the Manor of Norstead and all the lands belonging to it to his wife Bridget for life, with remainder firstly to his cousin Henry Skeggs, and then to Henry's son John and his heirs for ever.

Unusually for this period, Edward Skeggs did not make any conditions about his widow Bridget only enjoying the property while she remained his widow, and in the event she got married again very soon after his death, to Sir James Wolveridge or Wolrich. She seems to have enjoyed the property for many years, and Sir James must have died, because by the time of the lease of 1638 mentioned above Dame Bridget had married for a third time, and was then the wife of Robert Doyley of Lincolns Inn, gentleman. John Skeggs, no doubt the son and heir of Edward's cousin Henry, was still waiting for the reversion of the Manor and lands, a fact which is mentioned in the lease.

The Homage at the Court Baron of the Manor of Chelsfield presented in 1652 that Bridget the wife of Robert Doyley had died, and at last John Skeggs had come into his inheritance. To my knowledge this John Skeggs had first appeared in Chelsfield in 1632, when William Gilbert was indicted[5] for stealing from him a plough and coulter, value two shillings, but was found not guilty.

John had died by 1674, when Thomas Skeggs (perhaps his son, although I am not sure of the relationship) paid the Quitrent to the Manor of Chelsfield. He married Margaret Bodenham, the daughter of John Bodenham who owned Skeet Hill Farm. Thomas died aged 85 in 1717, and was buried under a ledger stone in Chelsfield church; he had no children, and in his will[6] all his estate went to his nephew, also called Thomas. As would be expected, he left money to the poor of Chelsfield and Cudham, and also to those of Shoreham, Horton Kirby and Sutton at Hone, which would suggest family links or property in those parishes. The will is rather tantalising because, although it names many relatives, they are generally described only as kinsman or kinswoman. He sounds a generous person, one touching item being "to Thomas More a Barber my old friend for the particular love I have for him and in regard of his great poverty I leave an annuity of £10.8s.0d. at the rate of sixteen shillings every four weeks to be paid at Northsted." He also left "to Paul Pattison a poor boy now living with me £20 towards putting him out apprentice."

The will was proved on 1 April 1717 by Thomas Skeggs the nephew and heir, who evidently relished inheriting Norstead. In September of that year there was great activity when he held a Court Baron and also commissioned Richard Adams to survey

the estate. The resulting map[7] is a large and brightly-coloured record, on two sheets of vellum, particularly valuable as it shows the buildings in perspective, including apparent oast houses next to the hop garden near the house. There is also a spirited rendering of the Skeggs coat of arms, with mantling, helmet, crest and motto. Field names are shown, and there is a table giving the measurement of each parcel of land or wood in acres, roods and perches, over 571 acres in all.

Although most of the estate was in Chelsfield, part was in Cudham, and just over the border into that parish, in the field called Brick Kiln Mollands, appears a "brick platt and road and kilne." This was excavated in 1975 by members of the Kent Archaeological Society, when substantial remains were discovered of a building no doubt typical of many such small brickworks which formerly existed in the area.

Thomas Skeggs junior did not live long to enjoy his good fortune, but died in 1722 and was buried in his uncle's vault, when Norstead went to another Thomas Skeggs (relationship not known) who died in 1739. He is described in the Chelsfield Court Roll of that year as a Waterman, although in his will[8] he calls himself a Yeoman. Thomas Skeggs left all his personal estate to his younger son John, and all his lands to his elder son, another Thomas, who according to Hasted sold Norstead in 1785 to Godfrey Lee Farrant of Widmore near Bromley.

Arthur Waring states that Godfrey left an only daughter Margaret, married to George Bensted, who in 1795 took the surname of Farrant. In the Tithe map terrier (1838) and in the 1842 Rental of Chelsfield Manor Sir George Farrant is in possession, but by 1848 he had been succeeded by George Bensted Farrant. The whole estate comprising 645 acres was sold in 1879, and the purchaser was not "a Gentleman engaged in Business and fond of Pleasure Farming" such as the auctioneers had suggested, but someone much grander, the fifteenth Earl of Derby, who at that time was building up a large estate in West Kent.

The sale particulars[9] give a glowing picture of the estate and speak grandly of the "Manor or reputed Manor with its Rights, Privileges and Immunities," although the effect is rather spoilt by the admission that "the Quit and other Rents arising out of the Manor (so far as can be ascertained) amount to £1.12s. per annum." The whole estate was then let to Mrs. Ann Phillips and Mr. James Phillips for a term of 21 years from Michaelmas 1860 at £500 per annum.

The Phillips family, who originated in Downe and have a family vault and other memorials there, were prosperous farmers in this neighbourhood, and successive members were tenants of Norstead for many years. The will of Thomas Phillips of Norstead who died in 1816 aged 72 shows that he was able to leave substantial legacies to his eight children. He asked his widow Ann to carry on farming Norstead with their two sons George Waker and William Waker Phillips and with the advice of the eldest son Thomas "as I conceive the same together with Industry and Frugality and what I have given to them by this my Will will be a Provision and Maintenance for them respectively and enable them to maintain educate and bring up all my younger children who at the time of my death shall be minors in a manner suitable to their degrees respectively." Apart from being tenant of Norstead Thomas senior owned small properties in Downe and Chelsfield.

He was followed at Norstead by his son George Waker Phillips who died in 1858. His widow Ann and son James were the tenants in 1879. The elder son George was tenant of Hewitts, while his cousin Maria Eaton had married William Beardsworth Fox of Lilleys and Court Lodge Farms, so that between them in Victorian times the Phillips family and their close relations farmed many hundreds of acres.

By the time of the 1881 Census[10] Lord Derby's Agent William Hughes, a Welshman from Merionethshire, was living at Norstead with his family. William was one of the nine men elected from among 21 candidates to serve on Chelsfield's first Parish Council in 1894. By 1902 he had been succeeded as Agent by his son John Collins Hughes, but in 1909 the seventeenth Earl of Derby had taken the decision to sell the bulk of his West Kent estates. Norstead was included in the 1595 acres in Cudham, Chelsfield, Knockholt and Downe, divided into 20 lots, while there was a further large estate in the Tonbridge/Sevenoaks area.

The auction particulars[11] were luxuriously produced, and the text of the part relating to Norstead shows that the vendor had hopes of realising higher prices by dangling before prospective purchasers the bait that the estate afforded "magnificent building sites." There is a photograph of the Manor House, described as "a charming Georgian residence of Brick, Stucco and Ivy-clad Elevation." From a close study of the details given, it would seem that the house had no gas, no running water and therefore no bathroom or WC, but only one earth closet. Lot 6 comprised the house, the "commodious farm premises," stabling, seven brick and tiled two-storied cottages and nearly 540 acres in Cudham and Chelsfield, sold to Charles Schwier, of whom I fear I know nothing.

He did not stay long in possession, and the estate was sold again in 1916[12], the purchaser being A.W. Machonochie, who had already bought substantial portions of Lord Derby's estate. He was a wealthy tycoon, Managing Director of Machonochie

Bros. Ltd., and had been an M.P., and he had an impressive London address, 8 Porchester Gate, Hyde Park. Sir David Waldron Smithers commented wryly in his History of Knockholt that Mr. Machonochie was "only too well remembered by soldiers in the First World War for his tinned food known as Machonochie's Rations."

He died in 1926, and on 7 July 1927 the whole of his estate in Chelsfield, Cudham and Knockholt was put up for auction by direction of his Trustees. The particulars[13] show that he had owned 2369 acres in these parishes, including Fairtrough, Cacketts and Charmwood Farms in Chelsfield. The glowing description of Norstead states that "the house which is substantially built and faced with rough cast with tiled roof, was at considerable expense thoroughly renovated by the late owner some years ago, when the interior accommodation was rearranged and modern conveniences were added." Two bathrooms are mentioned, one on the second floor being for the servants, while "Main Water is laid on, Electric Light and Bells are installed and the Drainage is conducted to a Cesspool on the property well removed from the house."

This is a convenient point at which to leave the history of this ancient Manor. In some other parts of the parish there is a melancholy record of buildings demolished and farmland developed for housing, but Norstead is a happy contrast, the ancient house still there and the demesne lands surviving as beautiful open country to this day.

References

1 CKS U312/T10.
2 CKS U47/11/T226.
3 CKS U71/M23. Other Manorial records seen are U36/M2,M42, U47/11/M25, M32, U71/M16-22, U86/M6.
4 PCC PROB11/112.
5 Kent Indictments Charles I, PRO publication.
6 PCC PROB11/557.
7 British Library, Additional MSS 38929.
8 CKS, Rochester Archdeaconry, Dra/PW9.
9 British Library, Maps 137a.7 (13).
10 RG11/857.
11 CKS, SP/385.
12 CKS, sale particulars XK/Chelsfield/SAV.
13 The copy I have seen is in private hands.

Chapter 14

THE PETLEYS AND THE MANOR OF HEWITTS

"To my dear friends and children having little to leave except my blessing I make no Will... "

-from Elizabeth Petley's "memorandum" 1818

The antiquity of the Petley family is emphasised by the strong, simple lines of their coat of arms. They were landowners and gentry in north west Kent from at least the 13th century living first in Downe and then beginning to acquire land in nearby parishes. John Petley, whose will[1] was proved in 1491, was an early member of the family to have lived in Chelsfield; he owned land called Symscroft and Wyche Haw Ridden, and left a ewe to the high altar, 2 ewes to the repair of the church, and a sheep to each of his godchildren. I am not sure of his relationship to William Petley who died in 1528, who has a brass memorial with figures of his wife and himself in Halstead church; he had become a man of considerable property, acquiring the Manors of Halstead and Hewitts in 1522. His will[2] also mentions his lands called Coalgates and Skypps in Shoreham and Halstead, and property in Chelsfield, Farnborough, Cudham, Otford, Knockholt, Bromley and Lewisham in Kent, and Beddington in Surrey.

Among the Petley estate papers is a petition by Thomas Petley, seeking to invalidate the will of this William, his father, which had been proved by Stephen, the eldest son. The accompanying evidence[3] recounts how this will had been discovered in a table in the hall of his house at Halstead, and Thomas contended that it was a forgery. He produced another one, which he said had been found in William's doublet, and although the evidence in the case is inconclusive, Stephen remained in possession, so it would seem that his brother's efforts to upset the will were unsuccessful. The sixteenth century was a prosperous one for the Petleys, who at that period owned some 500 acres in and near Chelsfield, including Hewitts, Gillmans Brimstone and Bucks Cross farms and land at Goddington and Green Street Green.

An inquisition[4] held in 1602 found that in the Bull at Otford "William Petlye of Chelsfield gentleman" – the owner of Bucks Cross - had stabbed Samuel Renolds of Maidstone in the chest with a dagger, inflicting a wound from which he had died the following day. William was indicted for murder at Dartford Assizes in February 1603 and was found guilty of homicide, but escaped punishment by being "allowed clergy" because he was able to read and write. An inventory of his goods included timber, rough and hewed ready for building (value 10s.), a frame for the roof of one end of a house (£1), and a number of animals including 30 lambs, 12 ewes and 10 wethers (£7).

The Petleys of Chelsfield were attached to their parish church, William Petley in 1599[5] for example leaving twenty shillings towards the "reparations" of the building. The story of the Royalist brothers Robert and Anthony Petley during the Commonwealth is told in another chapter.

It was soon after the Restoration that the first signs of a decline in the Petley family fortunes in Chelsfield began to appear. Robert of Bucks Cross died childless in 1668, and in his will[6], after providing for his widow, he left the bulk of his lands to his "cosen Robert Smith," with remainder in case Robert had no children to "my very loving kinsman Richard Thomas of Deptford gentleman." In the event, Robert also died childless and Richard Thomas and his heirs inherited.

Elsewhere in the parish too the hold of the Petleys began to slacken. Hewitts Manor and the lands belonging to it had descended to a Thomas Petley, and upon his death without

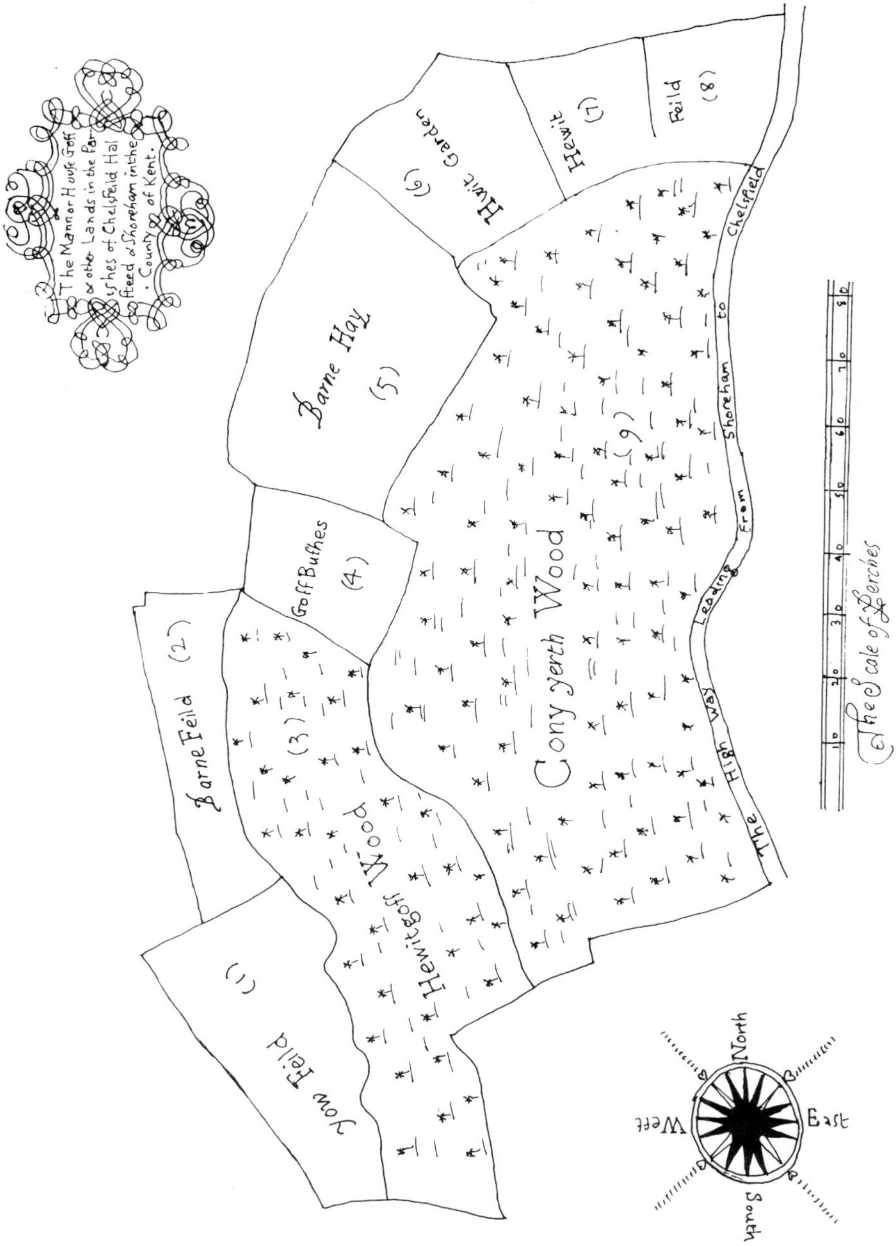

Hewitts Goss Farm, 1732 - a tracing by Susan Pittman from a photograph by Arthur Waring

issue in 1664 that estate was divided. The farmhouse and over 100 acres to the west of it were sold, but the family, in the person of Ralph Petley, retained the Lordship of the Manor, and some 80 acres of wood and pasture in Chelsfield, Halstead and Shoreham, known as Little Hewitts or Hewitts Goss, and he also kept possession of Gillmans Brimstone farm and about 70 acres.[7]

As shown in the Rentals,[8] the Manor of Hewitts claimed over a few properties only, scattered throughout Chelsfield, from Well Hill to Pratts Bottom. The annual quitrents amounted to about fifteen shillings, 2 hens and 10 eggs, but here, as in the Manor of Norstead, a Heriot (the best live beast belonging to the tenant) was demanded on every death or alienation. By the eighteenth century it had become uneconomic to collect the quitrents every year, and arrears of up to 39 years are mentioned in the Manorial records, but it was otherwise with the Heriots.

Robert Allen, the Petleys' tenant, paid £24 per annum for Hewitts Goss Farm in 1728, and in addition he was required to deliver one and a half good loads of cord wood to his landlord every year. He also acted as a Manorial agent for the Petleys, being responsible for searching out any beasts which would qualify as Heriots, marking them and seizing them for the Lord's use. It was customary for such beasts to be redeemed by the owners for a composition, or cash payment.

Parts of a detailed account book[9] for the Petley estates in Kent 1728-1742 have survived, showing that at Hewitts between 1729 and 1742 £28.5s.6d. was collected in lieu of Heriots. The following extracts show the working of the system, which must have made Robert Allen unpopular with the other inhabitants concerned:

1734 September 12: received there by Mr. F. Austen [the Manorial steward] and before by my sister of ... Ebbut, Burton and Aynscombe the Heirs of Mr. Stiles for 3 Heriots upon their alienating the lands lying in this Manor to... Fuller of Skid Hill - £6.6s.0d.

1734 November 9: to Money paid Robert Allen for his trouble in Marking a Horse of Mr. John Goodey's and three others of Mr. Burton Ibbot and Aynscombe when they alienated their Land - £1.1s.0d.

Buck's Cross Farm by John Cole, 1945

The Petleys did not live in Chelsfield after the death of Robert of Bucks Cross in 1668, and Ralph Petley who eventually inherited the Manor and Hewitts Goss Farm together with Gillmans Brimstone lived at Riverhead in Sevenoaks. When he died in 1751 the Chelsfield properties went to a cousin, Charles Petley, who was Storekeeper of the Ordnance at Chatham. The family kept its status of minor gentry, but the earlier robust connection with the land began to slip away.

Detailed abstracts of title to both Gillmans Brimstone and Hewitts have survived, the former[10] from 1694 to 1806, the latter[11] from 1752 to 1826. Charles the Storekeeper died intestate in 1765 and his widow Elizabeth administered his estate. There was a complicated deed of division in 1783, because of the property "being in the nature of Gavelkind Lands prevailing in the said County of Kent" so that it had to be divided equally between the coheirs, Charles's two sons

Ralph Robert Carter Petley and John Petley. The deed sets out that the brothers had come to an agreement to make "a Perfect Partition and Division between them" and Gillmans Brimstone was allotted to John, while the Manor of Hewitts, Hewitts Goss Farm and the residual 80 acres belonging to it went to Ralph, who had to pay his brother £21.6s.3d. to adjust the value of the division. John died in 1792 and left Gillmans Brimstone to his mother, who sold it in 1806.

The abstract of title to Hewitts Goss Farm and Hewitts Manor recounts a story which is full of human interest. Ralph Robert Carter Petley began a family connection with Scotland by his marriage to Elizabeth daughter of Dr Alexander Campbell in 1778, but died young ten years later. His eldest son Charles Carter Petley had an estate entailed on him, based on the family home at Riverhead. The two younger brothers Horace and John Cade Petley, who inherited Hewitts subject to their mother's life interest, both entered the services, and their destinies were very different.

John Cade Petley, who had been born in 1783, served in Spain, where he married Louisa Valverde de Calderon and became a Lieutenant Colonel in the Royal Artillery. Horace, who entered the Navy but never proceeded beyond the rank of Lieutenant, cuts a sad figure. I first came across his name in the "testamentary memorandum" of his mother Elizabeth Petley of Riverhead dated 1818[12].

She held Hewitts Manor and Hewitts Goss Farm for life, being described in the Manorial documents as the Lady of the Manor, and in her home-made will she comes over as a delightful, warm-hearted if somewhat woolly-headed person. Indeed, her brother in law Philip Cade had in 1798 left in his will[13] "to my sister in law Elizabeth Petley junior £20 for a ring as a token of my gratitude for her great kindness and readiness to come to us in all cases of sickness and distress."

In fact, Elizabeth laid up some trouble for her family by her 'testamentary memorandum' not being properly witnessed. She added two codicils in 1825, a few months before her death - the second one after realising that, far from having little to leave apart from her blessing, she had £500 3% Consolidated Bank Annuities standing in her name in the Bank of England.

In the first document she makes many gifts of personal items to near relatives, particularly her sister in law, Philip Cade's widow Elizabeth, whom she calls "my ever dear and beloved friend and sister Cade" who was left " my silver chain and bracelets and all my netting as being my work I know she will value. My diamond ring and watch I give into her charge to be given as she thinks proper either to Louisa, John's wife, or to any of my grandchildren when they marry or are capable of taking care of them..." and so on, remembering many relatives at great length.

The most poignant bequest reads - "To my beloved son Horace I return the watch which I have had in my possession under the hope that he will never part with it in the same manner again if he has any regard for those who gave it to him or to whom it once belonged. God grant that he may again be admitted into the society of his dear family and be grateful for their repeated goodness to him. My love and affection for him continues the same to the last moments of my life and I hope he will never feel as a parent what I have felt for him."

The story of Horace's financial problems is set out unemotionally in the Hewitts title, which recounts that, in addition to his share of his father's estate, and to five twelfths of the estate of his two sisters who died under age, he would be entitled to five twelfths of Hewitts Goss Farm and Hewitts Manor on the death of his mother. The title records that "Horace Petley became very embarrassed in circumstances and his aunt Elizabeth Cade from natural affection advanced considerable sums to him by gift to benefit himself and his family to pay his debts ..." A deed of 1811[14] shows that this same aunt generously paid him £1000 to satisfy any claim he might have under her late husband's will.

The abstract of title takes up the story - "Horace Petley again became in debt and Elizabeth Cade again agreed to relieve him" and in December 1822 he executed a deed settling on Trustees all the property he had inherited, or stood to inherit on his mother's death. It was recited that Elizabeth Cade "had advanced or was then forthwith to advance £412.10s. to the said Horace Petley as a gift not a loan to relieve him from his then embarrassments." An indication of how serious these embarrassments were is in a note written by Thomas James of New Court Temple about the draft conveyance of Hewitts - "evidence of the discharge of the debts for which Horace Petley was detained when he executed the deed should be given."

Poor Horace - who would seem to have been his own worst enemy - did not lack for support from his family; even his grandmother Elizabeth Petley, who died in 1822 aged 91, left him[15] £50 and an annuity of £50. He did not live long to enjoy this, and survived the mother to whom he had caused so much anguish by less than a year. When he had made his will[16] a little earlier he was living in Clerkenwell, and he left no personal legacies, referring only to the Trust set up in the deed of December 1822.

The title to Hewitts reveals that Horace was not the only member of the family who was having money problems. His elder brother borrowed a total of £2500 from various local tradesmen in 1823-25, which argues some pressing need, David Petley-Jones has suggested convincingly that the finances of the Petleys, from whom he is descended, had been badly affected by the collapse in 1818 of the Tonbridge Bank, which was owned by their relatives the Woodgate family.

The death of Elizabeth Petley in 1825 cleared the way for the disposal of the Manor of Hewitts and Hewitts Goss Farm, and it was agreed to sell the property to the Trustees of John Fuller, who in November 1826 acquired Hewitts for the benefit of his daughter Sarah, wife of Thomas Waring, the purchase price being £2788. The property continued in the possession of Thomas and Sarah's descendants, and their great grandson William Arthur Waring moved there after the sale of Woodlands in 1922. It and the other Waring properties were sold after William died in 1945.

As to the once powerful Petleys, their old farmhouse at Bucks Cross was rebuilt in the mid nineteenth century in attractive if utilitarian style, and is little changed in outward appearance. The venerable Gillmans Brimstone and Hewitts farmhouses have been restored as family homes, divorced from all but a little surrounding land. There are no monuments in St. Martin's church to commemorate the Petley family, and their memory is kept alive only by their coat of arms appearing on a beautifully embroidered modern kneeler there.

Julian (or Gillmans) Brimstone Farm
Drawing by John Cole c1945

References

1 CKS, Rochester Consistory Court DRb/Pwr6.
2 PCC, PROB 11/22.
3 CKS, U55/E40-42.
4 See "Kent at Law 1602" by Louis A.Knafla, PRO, 1994.
5 PCC, PROB 11/93.
6 PCC, PROB 11/327.
7 See Arthur Waring.
8 British Library 1710, 1723 Additional MSS 33,902: Waring MSS.
9 CKS, U55/E43.
10 Waring MSS.
11 CKS, U55/T92, combining an abstract of title and draft conveyance.
12 PCC PROB 11/1705.
13 PCC PROB 11/1325.
14 CKS, U116/T24.
15 PCC PROB 11/1655.
16 PCC PROB 11/1718.

Chapter 15

LILLEYS FARM – A WELL DOCUMENTED HISTORY WITH A TRAGIC END

"The residence is of the old-fashioned type so much sought after in these days by City men..."

-from the survey of Lilleys Farm, 1922

Lilleys Farm is often mentioned in these pages, because of the rich collections of material relating to the property, which have survived. In this chapter I will look briefly at the history of the house and the farm, and at some of its owners and tenants, and for once I will venture beyond my usual cut-off date of about 1920.

The first known owner was Peter Collet, Citizen and Merchant Taylor of London, who died in 1607. His memory is kept alive both by the fine monument to him and his family in St. Martin's church and by the Charity established by his widow Joanna, still funded by the income from Osborns Farm. In his will[1] Peter mentions that James Stile was then the tenant of Lilleys and that he was to be granted a further lease for 20 years at £24 per annum. In 1617 James bought one moiety (or half) of the farm from Peter's daughter Dame Hester Awcher and Sir Antony Awcher her husband[2]. At the time of the conveyance 120 acres of land in 14 parcels belonged to Lilleys, and most of the field names which are given also appear in the Tithe Map survey of 1838. These include Warly, Freese, Gravel Croft, North Grove, Wheat Field, Gray Hawes and Swiers.

James died in 1642, when his property descended to his son, another James, who came to own the whole of Lilleys by buying the second moiety from Sir Henry Heyman, who had married Peter's other daughter Sarah. James died in 1677 and his son and heir John Styles in the following year, by which time the family estate included not only Lilleys but also other property in Chelsfield, Farnborough, Lullingstone and Orpington. In his will[3] John directed that a house should be built on a piece of land called the Barne yard "that my sister Barbary Burton... shall have her dwelling in the said house gratis... provided she accept the said dwelling in lieu of the £4 per annum given her by my father's will." This house, in the angle of the road opposite Lilleys farmhouse, was later home to Thomas Bath (died 1746), a substantial inhabitant whose name occurs in the title deeds of both Cross Hall and Cross

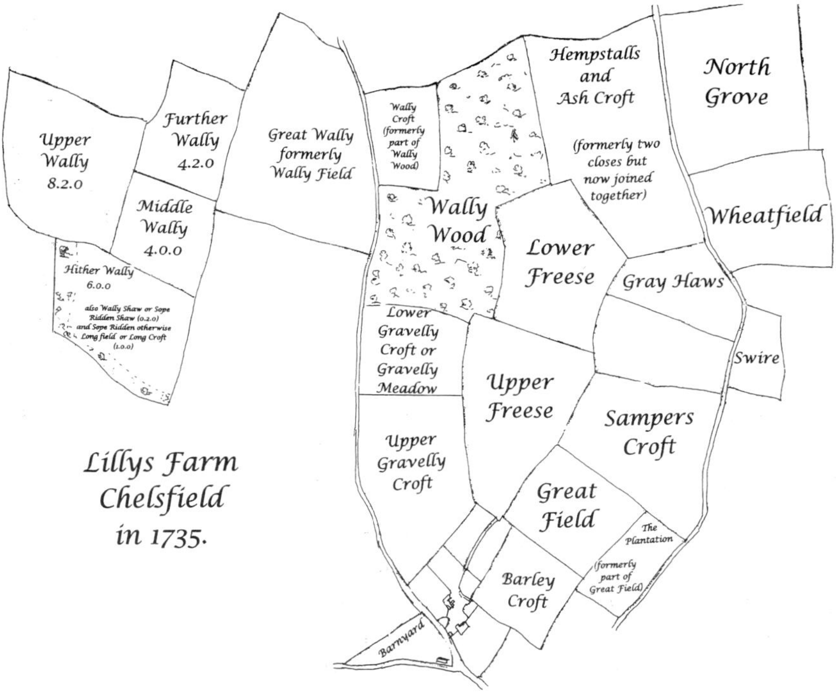

House as lending money on mortgage. The dwelling in the Barne yard was later rebuilt as a pair of cottages for farm labourers.

John left three sons, but because two of them died young all his lands descended to James, who was only about 11 when his father died. The story of the break-up of James Styles's estate is told in the chapter about the Chelsfield inheritance case. In the settlement of 1733 part of Lilleys was allotted to James Burton as his share, and he acquired the remainder by purchase, with the aid of a mortgage of £500. Oddly enough, John Petty who advanced the money was the Rector of Chelsfield's brother, about whom James Burton had made such wild accusations in the course of the costly inheritance case. It is evident from his will[4] that he was worried this might be a burden to his widow Susannah, who was left a life interest in the farm and allowed to live there rent free "and to have the use of a Bed Room and the fore Parlour therein during her life if she so pleases" but in the event the mortgage was paid off in 1754, two years before Susannah died.

James's daughter Barbara married Thomas Judd, and they lived at Lilleys after James died in 1741, Thomas farming the land himself. He died in 1786 and his wife in 1788, and as they had no children the ownership of Lilleys descended to her niece Mary who had married James Aynscomb, the heir to the Goddington estate. Lilleys (and also Goddington) came to the Harris family by the marriage of James and Mary Aynscomb's daughter Mary to James Harris in 1787, Mary inheriting both estates on her mother's death in 1793. James Harris died in 1837 and Mary in 1846, and in the division of the Harris estates between their three sons in 1847 Lilleys with 135 acres was allotted to John Harris. He farmed the land himself from 1850 to 1853, but thereafter it was always let, and John moved to Lillys Cottage, Bexleyheath, where he died in 1873.

He left Lilleys to his widow Selina for life, then to his Godson and nephew George St. Pierre Harris, but George had to wait until his aunt's death in 1907 to come into this inheritance. He was an Orpington architect, who from the 1870s onwards was responsible for much development in that parish, mostly on Harris family land; Aynscomb Angle is perhaps the best known. At Lilleys too, with the agreement of Selina, some 31 acres were sold, most of which remains open to this day, although Edward Norman of Chelsfield House built Orchard Cottages on one plot.

In 1922 a report on Lilleys was commissioned from R.A. Jack, architect and surveyor, who stated that "the older portion of the house, which is evidently of Tudor construction, is reputed to have been built in the year 1560 and contains some fine oak timbers and a king-post. The wing is said to have been added in the reign of Queen Anne and the house has been altered enlarged and modernised within recent years by the addition of a bathroom two lavatories, W.Cs. etc..." Interesting pencilled notes have been made on the plan attached to the survey, presumably by Mr. Harris. These include a faintly indicated "proposed road" to the north of the farmhouse, apparently leading through to Skibbs Lane and intended for a housing development, which did not materialise.

George St. Pierre Harris died in September 1939, leaving the reversion of Lilleys after the death of his wife and two sisters in law to his granddaughter Mary Aynscomb Llewellyn. After the farmhouse and cottages were wrecked by a flying bomb in 1944 the ruins and some surrounding land were bought by the brothers Dick and Bill Sanderson[5], who built Lilleys Cottages and a detached house on the farmhouse site, and another house on the opposite corner.

To return to the farmers who lived in Lilleys after 1788, Mary Aynscomb's first tenant was William Culver. I know nothing of him, but some scraps of accounts he sent to her have survived including, for example (in the original spelling) -

"1791 August 9: to 22 Bundles of thatching Rods - 15s.8d: to a hors and cart caring the Bushes a bout the Grown that Came from Godrington – 1s.0d. Nov. 12 to a man mending the heages After the timber Wagon – 1s.6d."

In 1792 Joseph Brooker become the tenant of Lilleys; he was a member of a prosperous family who have tombs in Footscray churchyard, and he had previously been the tenant of Cockerhurst Farm near Well Hill. The lease of 1792 is lost, but when it was renewed for 21 years in 1809 he agreed to pay an annual rent of £100, for a total of 120 acres and also land called Londridge in Great Smallams and the cottage "at or near Lilleys Cross." A charming watercolour of Lilleys from the northwest, painted during Joseph Brooker's tenancy in 1828, has survived in his family, showing a neat front garden and, to the right, a substantial brick-built dovecot. This had been demolished by the time of the 1868 Ordnance Survey 25" map.

The remarkable journal of Joseph's son Samuel Brooker, who followed him as tenant of Lilleys, was intended primarily as a record of work on the farm. David Squire, who is Samuel's great great nephew, very kindly entrusted me with the volumes to photocopy and transcribe. This is no mean task, as Samuel made an entry of at least a couple of lines every single day, starting at Old Michaelmas (11 October) 1836. So far I have transcribed only the first two years, running to some 90 pages of typescript – but Samuel really deserves a whole book to himself. I sent copies of my transcript to Dr. Joan Thirsk, the eminent authority on agrarian history, who commented that she did not know of any diary comparable in its degree of farming detail, adding "one does not get from it much of a view of the farmer's personality, but the farming routine is superbly recorded."

Samuel made a note of weather conditions every day, and each Sunday he gave the text of the sermons he heard preached, generally at Chelsfield. He had quite frequent social outings, noting for example in February 1841 that he "went to Northstead to a quadrille party with Mr. J. and Misses Ray. In consequence of the severity of the weather borrowed Gear's 4-wheeled fruit van. During the evening a high wind drifted the snow so as to require the assistance of 4 carthorses – very pleasant party. Total eclipse of the moon." In July 1843 he "went to Mr. Spain's Court Lodge to Quadrille Party – tremendous storm accompanied with thunder and lightning, which lasted from 12 to 3 in the morning."

Samuel was an eligible bachelor, and only thirty when he began the journal, but there is little mention of any close interest in the opposite sex. In contrast to his many laconic references to local inhabitants, his comments about animals, particularly horses, are positively poetic, as shown by the following entry –

"1847 May 10 – Little Bay riding horse died – bought of Mr. Fisher in October 1843 and was 8 years old – his qualifications as a hunter and a hackney together with a good temper justly endeared him to his Master and consequently his loss was much regretted by him as also by the whole neighbourhood with whom he was a general favourite."

Finally, here are two typical entries about his farming and other activities -

"1837 July 26. Team plough in Upper Warley – 5 men

gathering cherrys – went to Northstead – Cricket Club met at Chelsfield for the 1st. time [6] – Mr. R. Snelling paid for my wheat – very fine day Wind S.
1838 August 4. Team ox and smallharrowed part of Gravelcroft – sowed rape in Do. Men raking off cooch in do. – went to Deptford and Dartford Market – wheat white 78s. Pr. Quarter – red Do. 74s. Mr. Colgate called – showery day – Wind SW."

Samuel Brooker gave up the lease at Michaelmas 1850 and moved to Tubbendens in Farnborough. Two Inventories were drawn up, one covering fixtures, furniture and effects in the house in great detail, and the other "the Hay, Straw, Haulm, Seeds, Ploughings, Harrowings, Rollings, Growths of Underwoods, Erections, Half Dressings, Labor to Manure and effects..." about the farm. John Harris his landlord took the opportunity to buy a number of lots when Samuel held an auction of unwanted goods, and paid £331.11s.0d. for the items in the second Inventory, which James Russell of Horton Kirby and William Stow of Farnborough Hall had appraised. Samuel noted that he "sold Chestnut Chaise Horse to Mr. Darwin of Down."

At Michaelmas 1853, a new era opened in the history of Lilleys, when John Harris let the house and farm with 135 acres to William Beardsworth Fox of Downe for a term of 21 years at £155 per annum. The lease is an immensely long document with many covenants relating to the farming of the land and the upkeep of buildings, and includes one that "the tenant shall not lop top or trim the lime trees near or at the west end of the garden." There is a lengthy schedule of fixtures and fittings, including in the kitchen "a 48 inch kitchen range with oven and boiler behind ... a wind-up roasting jack with pullies, lines, cast iron weights and case."

William Beardsworth Fox was born at Hatfield, Hertfordshire in 1816, the son of John Fox who shortly afterwards moved to Kent, where he established Fox's Brewery on the Farnborough side of Green Street Green. William's brothers John Woodhams Fox and Thomas Samuel Fox carried this on, and he took no part in the business. Instead he became very successful as a farmer, eventually taking on the tenancies of the Court Lodge and Bucks Cross lands in addition to Lilleys. No doubt the several hop gardens on his land would have helped to supply his brothers' enterprise.

William was one of only three Liberals out of 26 voters in Chelsfield in the 1865 West Kent election, and he was also a devoted Methodist, two things that often went together. He was a leading spirit in the building of the Wesleyan chapel at Chelsfield in 1872[7], but was no bigot. When Chairman of the meeting held at the opening of the chapel he was reported as saying that he hoped that the day was not far distant when he should see the Rector in the chair instead of him. The Rector in turn, writing[8] to the Archbishop, described Mr. Fox as "a zealous dissenter" and said, "the Wesleyans who regularly attend their Chapel services are some of the best respected people in the parish." Mr. Fox's elder son Edwin met an unhappy end in 1893, when the horse pulling a water barrel, which he was driving to Well Hill, trampled him. When William Beardsworth Fox died in 1896 he was succeeded at Lilleys by his younger son – always known as "Willy" Fox. He renewed the lease for 7 years in 1905, and after his retirement in 1912 he and his sister Kate who kept house for him enjoyed a long Indian Summer at Hollycroft at Maypole, both of them living until 1945.

When Mr. Fox gave up the farm, Mr. Harris decided to let the house and close on 8 acres immediately around it separately from the bulk of the land, Herbert Birch being the first tenant, followed in 1919 by Clarence Frank Leighton. The farm lands, then reduced to 96.314 acres, with the farm buildings and the labourers' cottages, were let for 14 years to David Longlands Pattullo of "Yarrow" in Orpington, at £120 per annum.

At the end of his lease a "Record under the Agricultural Holdings Act" was taken, revealing an unsatisfactory state of affairs. The surveyor's conclusion was that "the greater portion of the Arable land is in a very neglected and foul state of cultivation. There are no gates at all on the land, but the fences are generally well laid and serviceable." Among the buildings, a pair of "brick, cement foundation and galvanised exterior cottages", which had been built on a site behind the present Lilleys Cottages, was in a particularly bad way.

The new tenants, William (otherwise Walter Joseph) Hoeltschi and George Hoeltschi of Orpington signed the report as an acknowledgement of the state of the farm when they took over, their lease being for 21 years from Michaelmas 1926 at £205 per annum. Walter became sole tenant in 1932, and gave up the lease in February 1939. A lasting memento of the Hoeltschi tenancy is that Lilleys Wood is known to older inhabitants to this day as "Oshi's Wood".

It should be possible to find detailed reports about the way in which Lilleys was farmed during the War, in the records of the Farm Surveys undertaken in 1941-43. I have photocopied the 6" scale OS maps on which the various Chelsfield holdings were plotted[9] but unfortunately a group of the surveys[10] from the parish, including that for Lilleys, have either been lost or, more likely, misfiled, and I can only hope that they will resurface.

Sketch of Lilleys Farm after being hit by a doodlebug by John Cole, 1944

The last tenant of Lilleys farmhouse was Frederick Chapman who was a dog breeder. In 1944 the Germans' flying bomb (or doodlebug) offensive was launched and late in the afternoon of 27 June 1944 the young Bob Hogben and Bryan Yates were at the bottom of Rock Hill when they saw a RAF aeroplane tip a doodlebug, which appeared to them to land near Bucks Cross Farm. They ran there, but everybody was heading towards Chelsfield Lane, where they found the devastated Lilleys, with several Special Constables headed by Mr. Waring at the scene. Mr. Chapman and his wife Edith had been killed, but luckily for the kennel maid it was her day off. She came and did what she could for the dogs, but some had been killed, and others had to be put down. The remainder had to be found homes, Ruby and Eddy Miller of Court Lodge Farm taking a black cocker spaniel which they called Doodle.

The only other recollection I have gathered is of a near miss. Marjory Smith (née Bowen) who had been to an afternoon class in the schoolroom behind the Methodist chapel was cycling home on what she recalls as a beautiful summer afternoon when the bomb fell, causing a cast-iron ventilator to fall from the ceiling into the room they had just left. Philip Lane records that the row of old lime trees had their leaves and some branches removed by the blast but, remarkably, survived, while for many years the old jet tube from the flying bomb rested in the corner of Lilleys Wood. The blast blew out parts of the east windows of St. Martin's, and when they were completely replaced some years later I salvaged a few diamond-shaped pieces of the Victorian glass, unfortunately lost when we moved from Orpington in 1960.

References

[1] PCC, PROB11/111

[2] Unless otherwise stated, all of the documents quoted are among the Harris Manuscripts, my catalogue of which is in Bromley Local Studies Library.

[3] CKS, Rochester will Dra/PW3.

[4] PCC, PROB11/716.

[5] Clare Hogben, Dick Sanderson's daughter, has kindly given me a 1947 deed with map of the destroyed buildings and the surrounding land, and also plans of Lilleys Cottages by George Rose of Chelsfield Hill, the architect of the Village Hall.

[6] Although cricket was played here at least from 1734, this is the first reference I know to a Chelsfield Cricket Club.

[7] See the history of Chelsfield Methodism, 1912, in Sevenoaks Local Studies Library.

[8] Visitation papers. VG 3/4a (1872) and VG 3/5a (1876).

[9] PRO, MAF73/20/16.

[10] PRO, within MAF32/1033/92.

Chapter 16

CHELSFIELD AND THE GREAT WAR

"While we shall sorely miss our dear and only boy, we know his death was a glorious one..."

- reported words of the parents of Private Oliver Corke of Well Hill, August 1916

Fifty two young men from Chelsfield were killed in the Great War, out of a total population of some 2000, and for many years the only monument to them was a framed, homemade list in the porch of St. Martin's church. The Rev. Norman Woodhall became Rector in 1951 and soon had a permanent monument erected there, to the memory of the dead of both World Wars[1] . I wish now that I had salvaged the original memorial, which, as I recall, had a certain pathos and was embellished with watercolours.

The records of the Commonwealth War Graves Commission are now on the Internet, a great help when trying to identify the war dead. In many cases however details are lacking, and much more information, including a photograph, may sometimes be found in the pages of local newspapers. As an example, one number of the Orpington and Kentish Times of August 1916 had obituaries of five young men from Chelsfield, all casualties of the Somme offensive. To illustrate what may be found I have followed up their stories, and those of other victims of the War.

That of Thomas Hopkins is particularly sad. In 1998 Mrs. Doreen Papa from Rhode Island, USA, wrote to Derek Sheffield about his books on Chelsfield. She is the grand-daughter of Thomas Hopkins (bailiff to Court Lodge Farm) and his wife Alice, and when a child she had often stayed with her widowed grandmother, at Station Cottages, Chelsfield. Doreen was coming on a visit to England and was keen to find out more about her family here. She knew that her father, Fred, had

had a brother, but she was puzzled that no one in the family had ever talked about him – what had he done that his name had been blotted out?

Clare Hogben looked into the story, and her mother, who had known the family well, provided the answer - the brother about who no one spoke was Thomas Hopkins, who had been killed in 1916, aged 20. His mother had been so upset at his death that afterwards his name was never mentioned in the family. Clare obtained details about Gunner Hopkins, of the 81st. Brigade, RFA, through Brian Cornelius, and she also consulted Chelsfield Parish registers. By the time Doreen came to revisit Chelsfield much information was ready for her, while later Mr. Cornelius photographed Gunner Hopkins' grave in the Military Cemetery at Carnoy, Somme, France.

More recently I provided a copy of his obituary, with a touching photograph showing a gentle young man in civilian clothes, wearing the cloth cap of the period. His portrait contrasts with that of the only officer in this group, Captain Maurice Asprey of the Buffs, looking very soldierly in his uniform, with Sam Browne belt. He was the son of George Edward and Florence Caroline Asprey of the Court Lodge, where he had been born in 1895. After a Public School education he had joined the Officers' Special Reserve before the War, so that he took up his commission as soon as hostilities broke out. His obituary states, "he had for some time been in command of a trench mortar battery, and was a young officer of great

Leslie Collins, portrait of a Great War soldier, circa 1917

promise." He is commemorated by a gravestone next to that of his parents in Chelsfield churchyard, but he is buried in Bray Military Cemetery, Somme, France.

Albert John Miles, the eldest son of Mr. and Mrs. Miles from the Shoreham side of Well Hill was a Rifleman in the Queen's Westminster Rifles. Before enlisting in the previous autumn he had been a butler in the service of Raymond Asquith, the Prime Minister's son, who was himself killed in action a little later.

Oliver Corke, the son of Thomas and Naomi Corke, who lived in one of the weather-boarded cottages adjoining the Rock and Fountain at Well Hill, was a Private in the Royal West Kent Regiment, who is buried in Combles Communal Cemetery, Albert, France. Did his parents really utter the brave words I have quoted, attributed to them by the Kentish Times reporter? I find it difficult to believe, but people then did have a simple sense of patriotism, which is less common today.

The last of the five men in this black week for Chelsfield was Frederick Checksfield, a Private in the Duke of Cornwall's Light Infantry, although in fact, he was then reported as "missing". His parents, Edward and Rose Checksfield of Hewitts Cottages at Bopeep, had had a letter from his C.O., who wrote that although he had no tidings to give them it was feared that their son had been killed or died of wounds. This was later confirmed, and Frederick is buried in Delville Wood Cemetery, Longueval, Somme.

Undoubtedly there are many other tragic stories hidden behind the bare names on the War Memorial. Mrs. Rhoda Cade of 1 Ash Road, Green Street Green, had to bear with the loss of both her husband Walter and her 19 year old son Edward. Sarah, the widow of Horace Chumley of the Scots Guards, also died, leaving young children who were brought up by relatives. One of the men at least, Lance Corporal Henry Kimber, son of Mrs. Esther Kimber of 2 Kingsley Road, Green Street Green, was awarded the Military Medal.

Also on Chelsfield War Memorial is the name of George William Smallwood, whose parents, Thomas and Annie Smallwood, ran the bakery at Cross Hall in Chelsfield village. He was a Private in the Border Regiment, and was killed in action on 26 October 1917, aged 26; as he has no known grave his name is commemorated on one of the panels in the huge Tyne Cot Memorial Cemetery at Zonnebeke, West-Vlaanderen, Belgium. I searched in vain in the Kentish Times for his obituary, and for those of several other Chelsfield men killed in late 1917, but none of them appeared, and I believe that this is because by that stage of the War casualty reports were censored.

Peter Beal of Crockenhill, George's nephew, has his photograph in a locket and a poignant greeting card, typical of many produced in France and Belgium for British servicemen. It is embroidered with a silk floral pattern and the words "to my dear Mother," and inscribed "with love and best wishes from your loving son George, France, July 28th. 1917."

Another victim of the War was Second Lieutenant Stewart Miller-Hallett, the son of Alexander and Amy Miller-Hallett of Goddington. He had joined the Public Schools' Battalion at the beginning of the War, and was commissioned in the South Wales Borderers in the summer of 1915. The Regiment was one of those involved in the long drawn-out battle of Mametz Wood, where Stewart was killed on 11 July 1916. His C.O. wrote that "he went forward with important information... and he did his duty bravely at a critical moment..."

He is commemorated in Chelsfield church by a stained glass window in the north wall of the nave. The name of the artist is not known, and in my opinion the design is at best undistinguished. The members of the Diocesan Advisory Committee were evidently not very happy with it, and a note by one of them on the Petition for the Faculty[2] reads – "NB – Before the application is granted I should like to know exactly what the design is intended to represent." Attached to this is a rather tetchy letter from Stewart's father, explaining that "...it represents St. Michael and his Angels overpowering the powers of Evil. You will notice, if you look at the sketch, that St. Michael has his feet on the Dragon and the Powers of Darkness are disappearing on the left hand side of the picture..." There was some further correspondence about the colouring of the proposed window, but the Faculty was eventually granted on 16 March 1920.

To turn to the home front, conscription had been introduced in 1916, and by the end of 1917 the Government was beginning to scrape the barrel in its efforts to fill the ranks. In an advertisement in the local paper in November 1917, the Bromley district Recruiting Officer listed the names and last known addresses of a large number of men aged from 18 to 40, inviting the public to inform him of their whereabouts. The fascinating list includes numbers of "van dwellers," while Thomas Lee, Joe Binkley or Buckley, N. Buckley and Henry Waller are all listed as having been last heard of at Court Lodge Farm, Chelsfield – presumably having been living in "Millers' huts" which were used by travelling farm workers. It would be interesting to know if these rather desperate measures succeeded in tracking down any of the missing men.

To finish on a rather lighter note, on 5 July 1918 the local paper carried the headline "CHELSFIELD RECTOR SUMMONED," about a case in which the Rev. J.J. Baddeley was hauled up before the Justices at Bromley for having ordered coal "in quantities exceeding two hundredweight in any one week without a requisition, contrary to the Coal Distribution Order." Mr. Baddeley protested that he had acted quite innocently and would not on any account break the law of his King and country; he was quite unaware of any such Order applying to Chelsfield.

The prosecuting solicitor pointed out that " the Order came into force in the preceding October, a copy of it was posted in the village, it must have been talked about and most of the leading persons in the district had filled in these requisitions, yet here was one of the leaders of the parish, a man of education and intelligence professing ignorance of a drastic Order made in the national interests at a most critical time... There was a tremendous leakage of coal; thousands of tons were leaking which the Coal controller could not put his hands upon."

Mr. Baddeley said he had not seen the Coal Distribution notice published opposite the Stone house, and his solicitor submitted that it was a purely technical offence. In a rather obscure reference he suggested that if the controller wanted to stop the coal leakage "let him go and look in the cellars of German barons of the country..." Poor Mr. Baddeley! - the Bench decided that he really could not be allowed to plead ignorance, and he was duly fined £10, his suppliers were fined £5, and each party had to pay two guineas costs.

The case casts an interesting sidelight on the quantities of coal consumed at that time. The old Rectory was a fair-sized house with seven bedrooms, and the Rector in evidence mentioned that it had been his custom to order ten tons of coal in April and ten tons in October every year; no wonder we used to suffer from smog.

"Homes fit for heroes" was Lloyd George's election slogan in 1918, and Council houses were built in small numbers in the parish during the twenties, at Green Street Green, Pratts Bottom and Bopeep. Kilnfields at Bopeep consisted of three blocks of four houses, with bath and inside lavatory – hitherto almost unknown luxuries in the village area, where outside privies were general for many years to come.

For the landowning classes, the old social order crumbled. The beautiful Goddington estate was broken up and sold piecemeal, and Arthur Waring of Woodlands had to sacrifice some of his family's property. Distancing future development as far as possible from the village he sold Julian (or Gillmans) Brimstone Farm to Homesteads Ltd[3] in February 1920. In what was definitely a buyers' market, the price agreed for the farmhouse and 219 acres of land, all situated beyond the railway line, was only £8000.

References

[1] The Village Hall built in 1953 also commemorated the dead of both Wars - see "Bromley's War Memorials" by Paul Rason, a copy of which is at Bromley Local Studies Library. Published in 2000, this 5 volume work has photographs and descriptions of all known War Memorials from both conflicts in the present London borough, and lists the names of all those commemorated.

[2] CKS, Rochester Diocesan Faculty papers, uncatalogued.

[3] For the subsequent development by Homesteads see the Chelsfield Park Millenium booklet edited by Paul Venton

BIBLIOGRAPHY

Printed books & booklets

It is surprising how much has been published on Chelsfield or Chelsfield families, in addition to the standard works of Hasted, Ireland and Greenwood.

1 A guide to the Church of St. Martin-of-Tours by John S. Barnes, 1981. Reliable and well-illustrated, including sketches by G. Roland Smith and Frances Peach.

2 The history of St. Mary's Church in Green Street Green by Marjory Love, 1987. Well researched, partly from Chelsfield Parish Magazines.

3 Pratts Bottom, an English village by Judith Hook, 1972. Written when the author was still at school, and containing some unusual information.

4 Asprey 1781-1981 by Bevis Hillier, Quartet Books, 1981. A history of the great family firm of jewellers, some of whom lived at Chelsfield Court Lodge.

5 Early Days by "Miss Read" (Dora Saint), Michael Joseph Ltd., 1982. Recollections by the well-known author of her childhood in Chelsfield, with charming line drawings.

6 Fragments and memories of an octogenarian by Philip Henry Hamblin, written 1978-81, published 1995. The author, a Methodist preacher, and publisher of the *Orpington Journal,* recollects life in Chelsfield and district from 1918 onwards.

7 Around Bromley a century ago, Bromley Borough Local History Society, 1985, has a chapter on Chelsfield by Peter Heinecke, particularly interesting on the village school.

8 In and around Bromley at the turn of the century, Bromley Borough Local History Society, 2000, has a chapter on Chelsfield by Geoffrey Copus.

9 Half-lights on Chelsfield Court Lodge by Alexander Theodore Brown, privately printed, Liverpool, 1933. Contains much original material on the Morland and Crawford families of the Court Lodge, and family portraits.

10 The Book of Orpington by Dorothy Cox, Barracuda Books, 1983, has a section on Chelsfield.

11 Shadrach Blundell, his family and property 1580-1880 by

Dorothea Teague, Synjon Books, 1985, and second edition, 2003. A very well-researched book on the Blundells, a family of yeomen and lawyers from Surrey who fell on hard times in the eighteenth century, when one branch came to settle in Chelsfield.

12 This forgotten place by Derek Sheffield, Meresborough Books, *1993.*

13 And then there were none by Derek Sheffield, Meresborough Books, 1994.

14 Till the end of time by Derek Sheffield, Meresborough Books, 1995.

This trilogy is also about the Blundell family, and has made the hamlet of Maypole familiar to a wide public. The late Derek Sheffield would not have claimed to be a historian in the formal sense, and his historical musings should be treated with some caution. However, his rumbustious recollections of the village in the thirties and forties give a vivid impression of life there seen through the eyes of a child and young man. There is a fine selection of photographs, and the third volume has a useful transcript of part of the Admission Register of Chelsfield village school, 1895-1945.

15 Pratts Bottom School Admission Register 1886-1917 by Roy Allchorne, Auckland, New Zealand. An excellent abstract of the register, containing much useful information not to be found elsewhere.

16 The story of Green Street Green School, 1851-1991 by Patricia Holmes, 1991. Well researched with many photographs.

17 Chelsfield Park Residents Association Millenium booklet, 2001 edited by Paul Venton. An interesting study of the development of this estate.

18 Skeet – a house in the country, an anthology edited by Allen Levy, New Cavendish Books, 1991. Skeet Hill House is in Orpington parish, but has close connections with Chelsfield. Since 1944 it has been run as a Jewish holiday home, initially for poor children from the East End. Excellent photographs – but beware the historical notes.

19 Centenary of Chelsfield Methodism, souvenir booklet by E.G.T., 1912. A mine of information, with photographs.

20 Calendar 1946 – 365 fact of History or interest in the district by Patrol-Leader Martin Lee, First Green Street Green Boy

Scouts. A notable achievement for a schoolboy of 15, including unusual items gleaned from old inhabitants.
21 Farnborough and its surroundings by J. Harland Blandford, 1914, has a section on Chelsfield, largely based on Hasted but with a little original information.

Other works, hand-written or typescript
1 Chelsfield Parochial Notes, 1912, by Arthur Thomas Waring of Woodlands, Chelsfield,(1851-1920), barrister, J.P., the first Chairman of Kent County Council, an Alderman and a member of the Kent Archaeological Society.
Two volumes, with many photographs and transcripts of documents, hand-written by him three times, with slight variations. One copy was presented to St. Martin's church and remains in their archives (photocopy at Bromley Local Studies Library). Mrs. Beth Nichols has another two-volume set, and volume two of a third set - I have photocopies.
2 Rentals and Rent Rolls of the Manors of Chelsfield and Hewitts, by Arthur Thomas Waring, c1912. Original with Mrs. Beth Nichols – I have photocopies.
3 Pedigree of the Kent Warings; Pedigree of the Fuller family by Arthur Thomas Waring, no date, c1912, very detailed. Originals with Mrs. Beth Nichols – I have photocopies.
4 Historical survey around Chelsfield from Paleolithic Age to 1940, by Patrol Leader Martin Lee, 1st. Green Green Scout Troop, aged 15, 1945, typescript. Another surprisingly mature work, including interesting comments, and reminiscences by old inhabitants.
5 *The Journal of Samuel Brooker*, 1836-69, four volumes. Samuel Brooker was the tenant of Lilleys Farm from 1836 to 1850, and then of Tubbendens, Farnborough. The journal belongs to Samuel's great-great nephew David Squire and I have photocopies: it is a major source, a day-to-day account of farming operations, with many references to other aspects.
6 The Commons at Green Street Green and Pratts Bottom (1956):
Notes on Worlds End, Chelsfield, (1993): *Alexander Miller-Hallett and the presentation of the new organ to Chelsfield church in 1893* (1993) – typescripts by Geoffrey Copus in Bromley Local Studies Library.

Collections of documents in private hands, referred to in the text

1 *Waring Manuscripts*. So far as I am aware, the bulk of the Chelsfield and Hewitts Manorial documents remain with the family solicitors, although a few are at CKS, Maidstone or at Sevenoaks Local Studies Library. I have so far catalogued all known documents of the Manor of Chelsfield.

The large collection of Chelsfield title deeds was dispersed when the Waring estate was disposed of after 1945, and it seems probable that many have been destroyed. However, some have survived and appear on the market from time to time. I have acquired a number, and a large collection was bought by Norman Millard, who presented them to St. Martin's church when he left the parish. Many years ago my wife transcribed a list of c1880, giving brief abstracts of deeds belonging to William Waring, and from this and other sources I have reconstructed a catalogue of known title deeds.

2 *Harris Manuscripts.* This collection was lent to me by my friend the late Michael Nightingale of Cromarty. It consists of 224 documents relating to properties in Kent and Surrey belonging to the Styles, Burton, Aynscomb and Harris families, 1503-1914, the bulk of them referring to Chelsfield and Orpington. A further 24 deeds relating to Lilleys, 1903-58, which follow on from the same series, now belong to Mrs Clare Hogben of Crosshall and have also been catalogued.

3 *Title deeds* of Cross House, Chelsfield, 1732-1959 were lent to me by Mr. and Mrs. David and Mary Lambert, to be transcribed and catalogued.

4 *Title deeds* of Cross Hall, Chelsfield, 1806-96 were lent to me by Mrs. Clare Hogben, to be transcribed and catalogued.

Copies of all my catalogues are at Bromley Local Studies Library.

A NOTE ABOUT THE ARTISTS

William Richard Cope lived in Orpington and taught art at the Regent Street Polytechnic. He worked in watercolour and oils, and also produced etchings of Orpington and district..

Frank Tilbury, an old school friend, was a structural engineer and a very talented artist who died in 1997. The drawing of Chelsfield village from the Recreation Ground was one of several scenes done for the Festival of Britain exhibition at Chelsfield in 1951.

John Cole is another even earlier friend from school days. His artistic talent blossomed very early, and I have included several sketches he did from 1944 onwards. A distinguished academic, and the author of a number of books, he is Professor Emeritus of Human and Regional Geography, University of Nottingham.

Heinrich Sigismund Uhlrich although born in Saxony was an inhabitant of Chelsfield village for many years – see chapter 9 for more of him.

(Arthur) Leslie Collins spent his childhood at Woodside, just over the parish boundary in Burlings Lane, Knockholt. He studied at the Slade School and exhibited at the Royal Academy when he was still young, and was also a prolific book illustrator. In the Great War he enlisted in the Artists' Rifles, and was killed at Oppy Wood in July 1917. I have the notebooks, which were sent back to his mother on his death, containing drawings including that of a fellow soldier - see chapter 16.

Dorothy Collins, his sister, was also a fine artist. She married David Owen and they lived at Hemsby, Worlds End Lane, Chelsfield for many years. It is possible that the drawings of the Bird Scarer and Gamekeeper are by her rather than by her brother.

Randolph Caldecott was a distinguished artist and book illustrator. In 1880 he married Marian Brind of the Court Lodge at Chelsfield church, and views of the house figure in several of his books – see chapter 11.

John Blundell, who drew the two pictures of the interior of Chelsfield church, studied at the Slade School of Art, and taught art in Sunderland and Inner London. He has written and illustrated guides to St. Mary Cray church and the Cray Valley.

ABBREVIATIONS

Arch. Cant. – Archaeologia Cantiana, the proceedings of the Kent Archaeological Society, 1858 to date.
BLS – Bromley Local Studies Library.
CCA – Canterbury Cathedral Archives.
CKS – Centre for Kentish Studies (Kent County Archives), Maidstone.
FRC – Family Records Centre.
LPL – Lambeth Palace Library,
PCC – Prerogative Court of Canterbury.
PRO – Public Record Office (now known as the National Archives).
Unless otherwise stated, references to Arthur Waring are to his Parochial Notes of 1912, while references to Samuel Brooker are to his Journal, 1836-1869 – see Bibliography for further details.

INDEX

LIST OF SUBSCRIBERS

Mrs	P	Ames
Mr	Keeling	Anthony
Mr	Stephen	Archer
Mr	John	Bailey
Mrs	Rosemary	Baldock
Mrs	Linda Carol	Barber
Mrs	Annie	Bardo
Mr	John S	Barnes
Mrs	Sheila	Barnes
Dr & Mrs	Probir & Jill	Basu
Mr	Peter	Beal
Mr& Mrs	Len & Anne	Beer
Ms	Heidi	Bergesen
Mrs	Janet	Binns
Mrs	S.	Bird
Mr	B.D.	Birks
Dr	Charles Alan	Biscoe
Mr	Tony	Blackamore
Mr	M	Blake
Mr	Harold	Blakey
Mrs	C.	Bourne
Mrs	Marie	Bowen
Mrs	E	Bowley
Mr	FH	Brabazon
Mrs	B E	Brett
Professor	Eric	Briggs
Mr	J	Brightman
Mr	George	Brooks
Mrs	J.E.	Budge
Ms	Jean M.	Burgess
Mrs	Sheila	Carr
Mrs	P	Carter

Mr & Mrs		Chandler
Ms	Anne Mary C.	Chapirson
Miss	R	Cheesman
Miss	Jean Caroline	Clapson
Mrs	DV	Clark
Mrs	Margaret	Cobbold
Professor	JP	Cole
Mr	LEW	Cole
Ms	Vera	Coomber
Mrs	Denise Christine	Coombes
Mr	Raymond Joseph	Coombes
Ms	Valerie	Cooper
Ms	Damaris	Copus
Mr	Matthew	Copus
Mrs	Doreen	Crane
Mrs	I	Crawshaw
Mrs	Jean	Crossfield
Mrs	Val	Curtis
Mrs	Anne	Davies
Mr	W.H.M.	Davies
Mr	David	Daws
Mrs	Sylvia	Dunford
Mrs	Jo.	Dunmall
Mr	M.J.	Dunmall
Mr	Dennis	Easy
Mr & Mrs	Jim & Rose	Edwards
Mrs	Jane	Eilbacher
Mrs	Linda	Fagg
Mr	Roger	Farthing
Mrs	Patricia	Fenwick
Mr	Simon	Finch
Mr	Peter D	Folley

Mr	William D	Folley
Mr	J.H.	Foreman
Mr & Mrs	Irene & Norman	Foster
Mrs	Jean	Fox
Mrs	Emerald	Frampton
Mr	Michael	Francis
Mr	Chris	Fruin
Mr	SR	Fuller
Mr & Mrs	C.H.	Gardener
Dr	P E	Gardener
Mr	Gordon R.F.	Gill
Mrs	M.	Godfrey
Mrs	Jan	Gow
Mr & Mrs	Paul & Irene	Gramann
Mr & Mrs	K	Griffin
Mr	Paul	Groombridge
Mrs	Mary	Haines
Mrs	Marion	Hall
Ms	J	Hammond
Mrs	Hilary	Harding
Mr	R	Harper
Mr	Duncan W.	Harrington
Mr	Alan	Hart
Prof	Gerald	Haslam
Mr & Mrs	Graham & Joan	Hayter
Mr & Mrs	SC	Heald
Mr	Peter M.	Heinecke
Mrs	Christine	Hellicar
Mr	Frank	Herd
Mr	W J	Hill
Mr	M	Hinton
Mr	Guy	Hitchings

Mrs	Clare	Hogben
Mr & Mrs	JA	Hollman
Miss	Joan	Holman
Mr & Mrs	Roger & Gillian	Hopkinson
Mr	P G	Horton
Mrs	Barbara	Howard
Mrs	Diana	Howden
Mrs	Phyllis	Hudson
Mr	Tim	Hughes
Mr	James	Hummerson
Mr	ER	Hurr
Mr	J R L	Ingham
Mrs	E.	Ivens
Mr	Sidney Mark	James
Mrs	Marjorie	Jelinek
Mrs	Florence E.M.	Jenner
Mr	Peter R.	Jones
Mrs	Brenda	Kealy
Mrs	Joy	Kelly
Mr & Mrs	Brian & Irene	Kemp
Mr	R.S.	Kempson
Mr	M.P.	Know
Mr & Mrs	David & Mary	Lambert
Mrs	Diane	Lambert
Mr	Philip A	Lamprell
Mr & Mrs	Philip & Jayne	Lane
Mr	Barry	Latham
Mr & Mrs	Philip & Margaret	Lawrence
Ms	Heather	Lawson
Mr & Mrs	Ken & Maureen	Lee
Mrs	Julia C	Lee
Mr	S.L.	McCann

Mrs	Freda	McClorey
Mrs	Madge	McLagan
Mrs	Anne	Mead
Mrs	ML	Meaden
Mr	AJ	Meddemmen
Mr	Michael	Meekums
Mrs	Carole	Mills
Mrs	Marion	Mills
Mr	RA	Mitchell
Mr	Bill	Morton
Mrs	Paula	Mourant
Mr	John	Mullen
Mrs	J	Mulvey
Ms	Penny	Mundy
Ms	Janice	Muraille
Mr	Colin	Murray
Ms	Joy	Nettleton
Mr & Mrs.	J.	Newman
Mrs	Beth	Nichols
Mr	John	Nightingale
Mr	Leslie R	Nurse
Ms	Sheila	Odgers
Mrs	P	Padgham
Mr & Mrs	Cyril & Mabel	Parker
Mr & Mrs	David & Julia	Parker
Mr & Mrs	Ian & Hilary	Parker
Mr & Mrs	John & Jenny	Parker
Mr	G	Parson
Mr	C.D.	Parsons
Mr	Jonathan	Parsons
Ms	Anne	Paterson
Mr & Mrs	Bill and Pauline	Payne

Ms	Marjorie	Peachey
Mr	Dave	Perry
Mr	Robert	Pfeiffer
Mr	John	Powell
Mr	RR	Price
Mrs	S M	Pritchard
Mrs	Margaret	Quilliam
Mrs	J	Randall
Mr	Brian E.	Ranson
Mr & Mrs	Paul and Denise	Rason
Mr	JM	Rawcliffe
Mrs	Marian	Reader
Mr	David A.W.	Redl
Mr & Mrs	Allan & Gwen	Reichert
Mr	Christopher	Richardson
Mrs	Enid	Richardson
Miss	G	Rickard
Mr & Mrs	JJ	Rooke
Mrs	V.E.	Satterthwaite
Mrs	Joy	Saynor
Mrs	Anne	Shearn
Mrs	Margaret	Simmons
Mr	Leonard G	Smith
Mrs	Marjory G	Smith
Mr	Sydney G	Smith
Mr	T	Smith
Mr	J	Spears
Mr	David	Squire
Mr & Mrs	B	Stambrey
Mr	Richard	Still
Dr	Alan	Stoyel
Mrs	S	Tanner

Mr & Mrs	John & Dorothea	Teague
Dr	Joan	Thirsk
Miss	Diane	Thomas
Mrs	DJ	Thorne
Mrs	Heather	Tilbury
Mr	Alan	Tompkins
Mr	Brian	Treasutle
Mr	Ray	Tuck
Mr	Karl	Turner
Mr	Bruce E	Venn
Mr	Paul	Venton
Mrs	Angela	Verrells
Canon	Leslie	Virgo
Mrs	Joyce	Walker
Mr	John	Ward
Col	H.B.H.	Waring
Mr	Philip	Warn
Mrs	Linda	Watson
Mr	Don	Welch
Mrs	ME	White
Mr & Mrs	John & Julie	Whybrow
Mr	Stan	Wickenden
Ms	Marjorie	Wigginton
Mr	Ray	Wigzell
Mrs	Elaine	Wiltshire
Ms	Hester	Woodcock
Mr	Bryan	Yates